Copyright © 1995 Royal Smeets Offset bv
All rights reserved

Editions of this book will appear simultaneously in France, Great Britain, Italy and the Netherlands
under the auspices of Euredition bv, Den Haag, Netherlands

This edition published by Magna Books, Magna Road, Wigston, Leicester LE18 4ZH, England

ISBN 1 85422 878 1

Translation: Tony Langham
Typesetting: Zspiegel grafische zetterij, Best
Printed in The Netherlands by Royal Smeets Offset, Weert

Production: VBI/SMEETS
Compilation: BoekBeeld, Utrecht
Design and text of plan, planting plan, flowering and colour scheme: Bureau Willemien Dijkshoorn BNT,
Amsterdam
Editor A-Z: Yvonne Taverne, Utrecht
Editor-in-chief: Suzette E. Stumpel-Rienks, Bennekom
Photographs: Plant Pictures World Wide, Haarlem
Planning and maintenance, text: Suzette E. Stumpel-Rienks, Bennekom;
Drawings: Theo Schildkamp, Haaksbergen
Small workers in the garden, text and drawings: Theo Schildkamp, Haaksbergen

This edition has been compiled with the greatest possible care. Neither the compiler nor the editor
accepts any liability for any damage as a result of possible inaccuracies and/or omissions in this
edition.

# Plants for Tubs and Patios

## Flowers & Plants

MAGNA BOOKS

# Contents

# Index

# Introduction

**A patio full of plants**

Over the past few years, container and patio plants have finally been attracting the interest they deserve. Containerised plants have found popularity with today's plant lover. Nearly all ornamental plants are now grown in containers, and there are thousands of varieties which, if properly looked after, will grow well in pots. The range of pots, tubs and troughs is also enormous, in terms of shapes, sizes and materials, and there is an appropriate container for just about every plant.

Container plants can be used in many different ways: in a patio garden, on a balcony or roof garden, in a greenhouse and even as temporary fillers for empty spaces in a flower bed. They are normally grown singly in pots, but well-chosen combinations of plants in a tub can also be very eye-catching.

Plants are very dependent on how they are treated and where they are placed. If not properly tended, they are likely to lead a half-hearted existence and come to a premature end.

True container plants come from the sunny south and cannot survive a northern winter, so will need to be overwintered in a cool, well-lit place. But even plants which are fully hardy in the border may not be hardy when grown in containers: after a few days of frost, the whole root ball may become a frozen lump of ice so that the roots can no longer function properly. Proper protection during winter may be the solution.

Many evergreen plants need a period of rest in winter, tired as they are after a season of growing and flowering. Container plants of any size are fairly expensive to buy, and most good-quality pots, toughs and tubs can also be fairly costly. But a well-balanced choice of plants and containers and a well laid-out patio will give you many long years of gardening pleasure.

However it would be wrong to think that an attractive patio garden is easy to maintain. Each plant will need specific care and attention, and the limited space in the container means it will need regular watering and feeding. But the advantage is that you can change the design from year to year as the mood takes you; even during the growing season it is easy to move the plants around to give maximum prominence to those that are in flower.

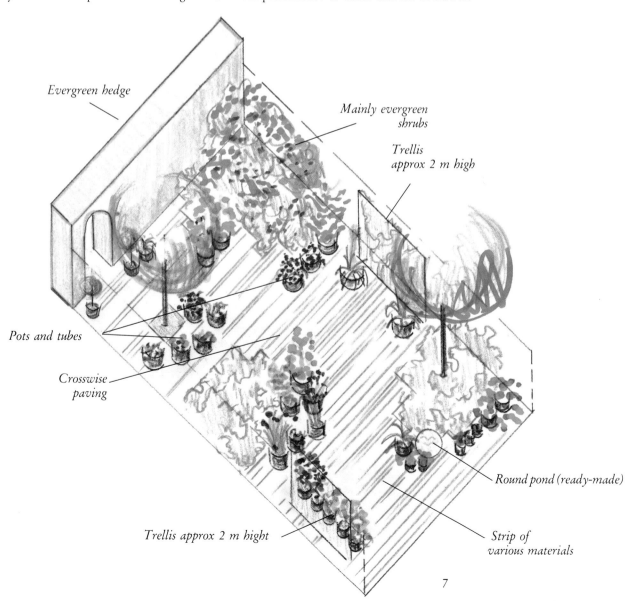

*Evergreen hedge*

*Mainly evergreen shrubs*

*Trellis approx 2 m high*

*Pots and tubes*

*Crosswise paving*

*Round pond (ready-made)*

*Trellis approx 2 m hight*

*Strip of various materials*

# The design

**Ground plan**
This patio garden is based on a combination of hard landscaping and planting. The combination is chosen so that there is plenty of room even without the container plants, so that it is primarily a patio garden but can also be used as a space for recreation.
This space can be gradually filled in with individual pots and tubs of plants.
The paving across the middle can be made from a diversity of materials: natural stone, brick, concrete tiles or combinations of these. Some practical hints have been given for the layout of the garden.
The planted areas are dominated by shrubs of various shapes and sizes. Two trees form the backdrop of the garden.
The hard areas have two trellis screens along the sides; these can be used to grow climbing plants and woody pot plants to create an eye-catching vertical element. The hedge at the end is tall and evergreen.
The small round pond is visible from the house and provides a pleasant touch; this has been obtained ready-made from a garden centre and the bottom filled with pond compost. Even without the addition of plants in containers, this is a relatively complete garden in its own right, though once the plants have been added the effect will be much greener.
It may require a great deal more hard work than it does now, but this "outdoor room" also becomes more flexible in its layout. Even during the growing season the plants can be moved around, and you can completely change the design every year if you want to, creating a surprising range of effects. And during the winter, there are some evergreens and hardy deciduous plants which will give you a pleasant view from the house.

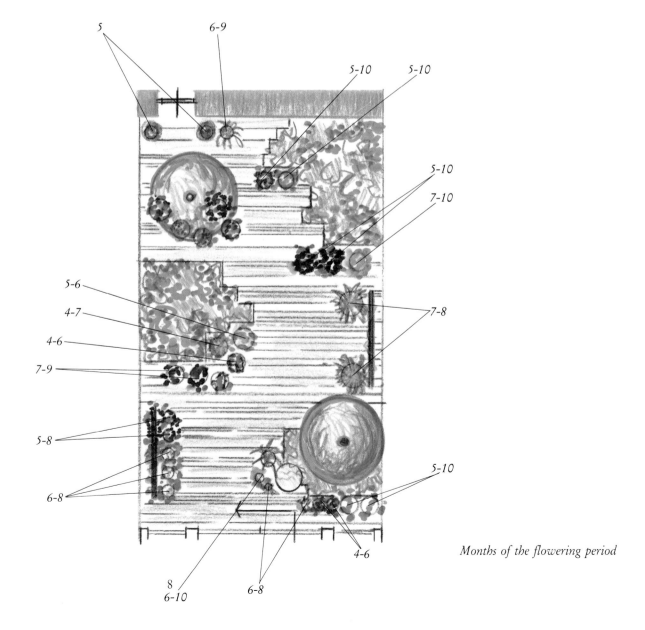

*Months of the flowering period*

# Planting plan

The plan for this patio garden largely consists of hard landscaping, with a few areas of open soil. These are planted with hardy shrubs so that there is something to be seen all year round. For planting suggestions for these areas, see the sections on "Beautiful flowering shrubs" and "Beautiful border plants".

Basically, the same rules apply to these beds as to the garden as a whole. They should have tall shrubs at the back, gradually decreasing in size towards the patio. The two trees, a sweet gum and a flowering cherry, both have globular crowns and reach a medium height of 5 to 6 metres. Although some of the plants are hardy, the design assumes that all the 30 or so planted pots and tubs are overwintered in a frost-free place.

The design of this garden is based on two main ideas:
– The plants in the borders provide a background for the distinctive shapes and colours of the container plants;
– The colours decrease in intensity as one moves away from the house, with neutral colours at the far end and a few bright accents.

Some of the plants are annuals and biennials, and will be regularly replaced by new or different plants. Biennials have two different faces: in their first year they mainly develop foliage, with the flowers not appearing until the following year. There is a regular succession of new plants and containers appearing on the market, but many of these date quickly. If a patio garden is not properly planned, it will soon become a colourful jumble of impulse-bought odds and ends. The small pond close to the house is at least 40 cm deep. It contains special pond compost, which is available in large or small packets.

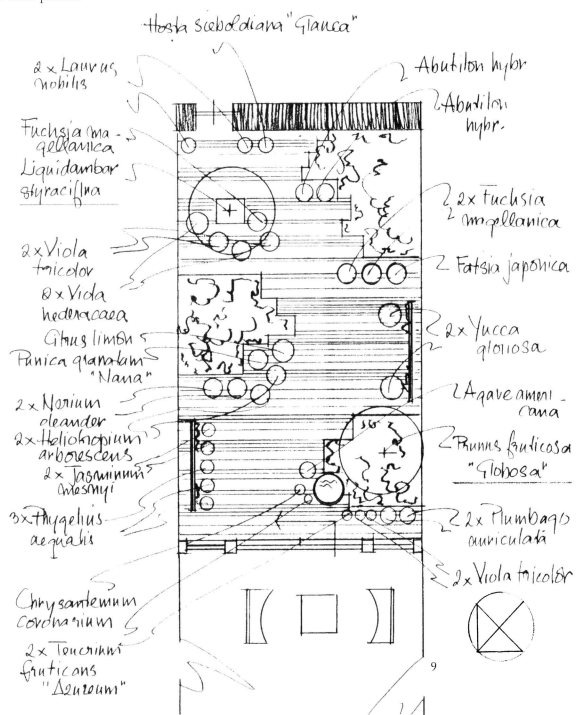

*Abutilon x hybridum*

# Abutilon

⚘ ↕ 0.60-2.50 m ⊘ ❀ 5-10 ⊔

*Abutilon* is indigenous in tropical and subtropical regions of Central and South America. This is a shrub with fairly limp branches and spreading, heart-shaped, palmate, indented leaves. The single, thin-stemmed, bell-shaped, red, yellow or orange flowers, consisting of five parts, grow in the leaf axilla and have striking, protruding, fused stamens. The flowers remain open for two days. Some species have variegated leaves.

*A. megapotamicum* has pendent flowers with a red calyx, yellow crown and almost black stamens; "Variegatum" has pale yellow, spotted leaves.

*A. striatum* (syn. *A. pictum*) flowers in August to September. This is a strong species, especially "Thompsonii", which has salmon-coloured flowers and yellow, spotted leaves.

*Abutilon* hybrids are crosses of different original species, usually with entirely green leaves, and yellow, orange, red, pink and white flowers; "Feuerglocke" has red flowers; "Golden Fleece", dark yellow; "Boule de Neige", white; "Ashford Red", brownish salmon-pink.

This plant is suitable for a light spot out of bright sunlight. Prune back in early spring and repot in normal potting compost; fairly small pots encourage flowering. It is necessary to tie back thin stems. Water liberally in warm weather; feed once a week. Do not feed in resting period (September to March). Winter, minimum 12° C; it can also be kept in a normally heated room. If necessary, pinch out tips at intervals for bushy growth. Propagate from seed and cuttings (top cuttings in spring) at 20° C.

*Abutilon megapotamicum*

# Acacia
*Mimosa*

🌿 ↕ 1.2-3 m ↔ 20-60 cm ○ ❀ (1) 4-5
✂ 🏺

The genus *Acacia* comprises many species, found mainly in the dry regions of tropical Australia, Asia and Africa. The name has caused some confusion; Mimosa for the genus *Acacia*, Acacia for *Robinia*, and in addition, *Mimosa* is known as the Humble plant. The species *A. dealbata*, *A. decurrens* and *A. baileyana* have produced many fragrant hybrids which are sold as cut flowers. This is a yellow, flowering, woody-stemmed, often thorny shrub or tree, with pinnate or compound leaves which fold up when there is a change in light or temperature.
*A. armata*, the mimosa tree, is a branching, thorny shrub with flattened leaf stalks and spherical, bright yellow flowerheads.
*A. baileyana*, Cootamundra wattle, has bipinnate leaves, abundant flowerheads in clusters 10 cm long; *A. baileyana* "Purpurea" has leaves with a purplish tinge.
*A. dealbata*, silver wattle, is a tree with bipinnate, greyish-green leaves, and fragrant, yellow clusters of flowers. It flowers early (January to April) and is excellent for cut flowers.
*A. longifolia*, Sydney golden wattle, has oblong, undivided leaves and clusters of flowers, 2.5-5 cm long.
*A. verticillata*, Prickly Moses, has needle-like leaves, and bright yellow clusters of flowers. It is resistant to salty sea winds, lime and wetness. This plant requires a light or sunny spot and soil rich in humus. Keep moist at all times, particularly in summer, though not too wet. Keep well aired. Feed liberally while it is growing. Overwinter in a cool place (4-6° C) to promote flowering. Prune immediately after flowering and repot if necessary in ordinary potting compost, pressing down the soil. Propagate from seed (spring) and stem cuttings (July to August) which form roots at room temperature.

*Acacia dealbata, Mimosa*

*Acacia verticillata, Mimosa*

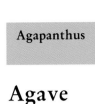

*Agapanthus orientalis,
African lily*

# Agapanthus
## *African lily*

○ ↕ 0.5-1.5 m ↔ 30-60 cm ○ ✿ 6-8 ✲ ▽ ▽

*Agapanthus*, which means "lovely flower", is indigenous in South Africa and comprises 10 species.
It is a herbaceous plant with fleshy roots, strap-shaped, dark green leaves, 40-60 cm long, and blue or white, trumpet-shaped flowers in umbels on long, bare stems.
*A. africanus*, African lily, has stems 60-90 cm long, with large blue umbels of flowers, and later, attractive capsules; there are also varieties with white flowers.
*A. campanulatus* loses its leaves. It is 75 cm tall and has pale blue flowers. It can also be grown outdoors; "Isis" has lavender flowers.
*A. praecox* does not lose its leaves and is sensitive to frost. It flowers profusely on stems more than 100 cm long. The leaves grow in rosettes and are 50-60 cm long, with large, light blue umbels; good for cut flowers.
There are many *Agapanthus* hybrids of various species, usually sensitive to frost, such as "Blue Giant", up to 110 cm tall, with large, blue umbels of flowers.
This plant is most attractive when a large group is planted in a tub in nutritious potting compost with some clay and well-rotted manure. It requires well-drained soil. Water liberally in summer, less after flowering, and keep almost dry in winter; do not feed. It will flower more profusely after many years in the same pot. It will tolerate a few degrees of frost and is resistant to wind. Propagate by dividing plant (spring) and from seed.
It attracts butterflies.

*Agave americana "Aureovariegata"*

12

propagation. To prevent injuries, put corks
on the points of the leaves while moving
plants or repotting.

# Arbutus
*Strawberry tree*

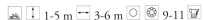 1-5 m ⟷ 3-6 m ○ ❀ 9-11 ▽

*Arbutus* is indigenous in southern Europe
and comprises only three species. It is a
shrub or small tree which is not really
winter-hardy, and has leathery, shiny green,
oval leaves with a serrated margin, panicles
of creamy-white, urn-shaped flowers, and
attractive, orangey-red fruits (from the
previous year) at the same time as the
flowers.
*A. andrachne*, Grecian strawberry tree, is
usually evergreen and up to 6 m tall, with a
reddish, flaky bark, erect flowerheads and
smooth fruits. This is a difficult plant which
is rarely cultivated.
*A. x andrachnoides*, a cross of *A. andrachne*
and *A. unedo*, has varying characteristics. It
often has spreading branches and a reddish

*Agave victoriae-reginae*

bark. It flowers for a long time and is
suitable for growing in lime-rich soil.
*A. unedo* is a moderately winter-hardy
evergreen, 5-12 m tall, with pendent,
orangey-yellow panicles of flowers and
rough, red fruits; "Rubra" has pink flowers;
"Rubra compact" has flowers with a pinkish
tinge. It forms runners and tolerates lime
well. It is suitable for a sunny, sheltered
spot, in acid, well-drained soil, rich in lime.
Water regularly, but not too much at a time.
Feed once a fortnight. Keep cool in winter
(5-10° C), with plenty of air and light.
Water less but do not allow to dry out; the
leaves must remain on the plant. Repot if
necessary. Propagate from seed
(March/April), by layering (July/August)
and from top cuttings (October).

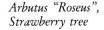

*Arbutus "Roseus",
Strawberry tree*

# Brassica
*Ornamental cabbage*

· | 20-40 ↔ up to 60 ○ ◉ ✿ 6-9 ▽

*Brassica* originally comes from
Mediterranean regions and temperate
regions in Europe and Asia. It comprises
many species and varieties. Many of these
are familiar vegetables, such as cabbage and
kohlrabi. In our own part of the world,
*B. nigra* is indigenous.
*B. oleracea*, ornamental cabbage, is an
annual with white flowers. In addition to
consumer varieties (kale), there are also
varieties with attractive coloured leaves; the
colours vary from green and white with a
yellow or red heart, to purple and white
leaves. They can have frizzy or smooth
edges.
In winter, they provide some colour in
windowboxes. They tolerate the cold fairly
well, but only slight frost. The colder it is,
the better the colours. Grow in the sun or
semi-shade in nutritious, well-drained soil.
Propagate from seed (mid-April to May),
thin out and plant out in August/September.

*Brassica "Keiho",*
*Ornamental cabbage*

# Brugmansia

○ | 1-5 m ↔ 2 x 2 m ○ ✿ 8-10 (all year)
! ▽

*Brugmansia* (syn. *Datura*), is indigenous in
Central and South America, and comprises
trees and shrubs. It closely resembles
*Datura*, Angels' trumpets, and was classified
under this genus in the past; it now includes
the more herbaceous species.
It is a poisonous plant with large leaves,
trumpet-shaped, often fragrant, pendent,
white, yellow or orange flowers. There are
also crosses.
*B. sanguinea* (syn. *Datura sanguinea*) has
dense foliage, and is 1-1.5 m tall, with oval,
soft-haired leaves. It flowers all year round,
especially in winter, and has orangey-red
flowers up to 20 cm long, which are not
fragrant.
*B. suaveolens* (syn. *Datura suaveolens*), up to
5 m tall, has oblong to oval leaves, 15-30 cm
long, slightly hairy on the underside, and
pendent, fragrant, trumpet-shaped, white
flowers, with a star-shaped margin,
25-30 cm long; "Plena" has double, white
flowers; "Rosa" has pink flowers.
Keep out of the reach of children. Because
of its fast-growing properties, it does best in

This is a very compact, evergreen, slow-growing shrub, with whorls of small, oval, oblong, shiny green leaves, and insignificant yellowish-green flowers in the leaf axilla. It is monoecious, which means that the male and female flowers grow on the same plant. *B. sempervirens* "Suffriticosa" is a dwarf variety with very small leaves; "Aureovariegata" has variegated leaves.

*Brugmansia x caudida "Grand Marnier"*

*Buxus sempervirens, Box*

large tubs of nutritious soil with loam and cow manure. In summer, it requires a sheltered, warm and sunny, airy spot. Water liberally, the temperature must not fall below 10° C. During the growing season, do not feed more than once a week. In winter, place in a cool spot (unheated greenhouse, approximately 7° C, young plants 10-15° C), fairly but not entirely dry. Propagate from top cuttings in a mixture of sand and peat (February, 20° C).

# Buxus
*Box*

🌿 ↕ 0.6-1 m or more ◯ ◉ ✿ 4-5 ❄ !

*Buxus* originates from central and southern Europe and western Asia. It comprises about 70 species, of which only one is widely cultivated.
*B. sempervirens*, common box, has been cultivated as an ornamental shrub for a long time. It is very easy to prune into shape and was therefore widely used in the 16th and 17th centuries for hedging and topiary work. The wood is very strong and is used to make rulers and handles for tools.

# Canna

⬡ ↕ 45-180 ↔ 40-60 ○ ❀ 6-10 🏺

*Canna* is indigenous in tropical and subtropical regions of America and Asia and comprises 55 species and a great many crosses.
This herbaceous plant has thick rhizomes, bright green, erect leaves, up to 60 cm long, and strikingly coloured flowers in red, orange, yellow, pink or white shades.
*C. indica* hybrids have been cultivated since the Middle Ages as decorative plants with profusely flowering clusters of yellow to dark red blooms. There are also varieties with bronze-violet leaves and multicoloured flowers; "Orchid", pink flowers; "Red King

*Callistemon, Bottlebrush*

# Callistemon
*Bottlebrush*

🌱 ↕ 1-1.5 m ↔ up to 1 m ○ ❀ 6-9 🏺 ✂

*Callistemon*, indigenous in Australia, comprises 25 species of trees and shrubs. The English name refers to the striking red or yellow clustered flowers which have no petals, but very long stamens.
This evergreen shrub has stiff, leathery, usually pointed, strikingly veined leaves, beautiful, cylindrical flowers, 10-15 cm long, and hard, grey fruits, close to the branches.
*C. citrinus* (syn. *C. lanceolatus*), the most popularly cultivated species, flowers at a young age. It has lanceolate, greyish-green leaves, which are lemon-scented when bruised; the flowers remain on the plant for two months.
This plant is suitable for a very light, sheltered spot, or indoors in a south-facing window with a lot of fresh air. Water moderately with tepid, lime-free water, spray occasionally and feed once a fortnight. Overwinter in a fairly cool place (6-10° C), keep fairly dry, not in a warm room. After flowering, prune back slightly, but not too much. New flowers develop on one-year-old stems. Pinch out tips of young plants. Repot every two or three years in acid, well-drained soil (coniferous woodland soil). Propagate from cuttings (August at

Humbert", bronze leaves and dark red flowers; "Richard Wallace", canary yellow flowers.
*C. x indica* "Lucifer" has bright red flowers with a yellow margin; it is a low-growing plant, also suitable for cultivating indoors. Suitable for a sheltered, sunny spot, for example, against a wall; harden off carefully in spring. Repot in April in potting compost with some sharp sand. Water liberally and feed once a fortnight. They like a lot of warmth, but will tolerate cooler nights (10° C). They continue flowering until the first night frost. Remove dead blooms. Keep in a fairly dry place at approximately 10° C for the resting period in winter. Propagate by dividing rhizomes in spring, in moist peat with sand, and sow in spring at 21° C after soaking seed for 24 hours. Young plants do not flower for two or three years. Watch out for snails.

*Canna indica "Lucifer"*

# Cassia

*Cassia Biflora*

 ⌄ 1-2 m ↔ 2-3 m ○ ⊛ 5-9 ⊔

*Cassia* is indigenous in (sub)tropical regions of America, Africa and Asia, and comprises about 500-600 species of herbaceous plants, as well as shrubs and trees. It is planted not only for its decorative value, but also for the medicinal uses of the leaves and pods.
*C. senna* and *C. angustifolia* have a strong laxative effect which has been used since the Middle Ages. In this part of the world only a few species are cultivated in tubs. The evergreen, aromatic leaves are composed of a number of pairs of leaflets on a straight leaf stalk; the flowers always have spreading yellow petals with protruding stamens and usually grow in large, erect or pendent clusters. The plants have long pods.
*C. corymbosa*, from Argentina, is a shrub, 1-1.5 m tall, with shiny green leaves and golden-yellow flowers in sprays;
*C. corymbosa* var. *pluryuga* (syn. *C. floribunda*), 1-2 m tall, flowers slightly later with smaller flowers, from July to the autumn; there are also small-leaved varieties with a tall trunk.
*C. didymobotrya*, Golden wonder, from Kenya, is a shrub up to 50 cm tall, which flowers all year round under good conditions. It has 4-18 pairs of finely-haired leaflets and erect spikes of flowers, 15-30 cm long. Cut back after flowering to promote new flowering. It does not have pods and cannot be propagated from cuttings. Overwinter at 12-15° C.
This plant is very suitable for a warm spot in full sunlight (unheated greenhouse). Protect against rain. Repot in potting compost with loam or clay and apply liquid feed once a week during the growing season. After flowering, prune back runners. Keep in a very light spot (to prevent leaves falling) in winter at 5-10° C. Propagate from seed (spring or August), and from semi-woody cuttings in summer, which form roots at 15-20° C.

top: Cestrum x "Newellii"

# Cestrum

⌇ ↕ 1-2(-3) m ↔-2 m ○ ◉ ❀(4-) 7-10 ⚠ 🪣

Cestrum, is indigenous in (subtropical) America and the West Indies, and comprises approximately 150 species. It belongs to the same family as food crops such as the potato, tomato and capsicum. This is an old-fashioned plant which is becoming popular again. It is usually a deciduous shrub or tree for the unheated greenhouse, with spreading, smooth-edged leaves, and small, tubular flowers, 1.5-2 cm long, usually growing in terminal trusses. It has red, white or black fruits.
C. aurantiacum is (semi) evergreen, with broad, oval leaves, 8-9 cm long, and orangey-yellow, fragrant clusters of flowers which open in the evening.
C. elegans (syn. C. purpureum), is (semi) evergreen with arching branches and pointed, oval to lanceolate leaves up to 10 cm long, with a rounded base, and purplish-red clusters of flowers.
Cestrum "Newellii" (syn. Habrothamnus newellii) is probably a cross of C. elegans and C. fasciculatum. It is an evergreen with crimson flowers.
C. parqui is more resistant to cold and has oblong, pointed leaves up to 14 cm long, and greenish-yellow flowers.
This plant is suitable for a sheltered, sunny spot, out of bright noon sunlight. It requires a lot of water during the growing period. Feed once a week. During the winter it has a resting period. Keep fairly dry, but the leaves should not drop off. 10-12° C; sensitive to fungus. Prune if necessary at the end of the winter resting period, and repot at the same time in ordinary potting compost with one-third part of lime-rich clay. Repot large plants every three to five years. Propagate from top cuttings in spring or summer. These take root at 20-25° C. The plant can also be propagated from seed.

Cestrum nocturnum

18

*Chamaerops humilis*

# Chamaerops

 up to 100 ◯ ⊘ ⊛ 5-6 🪣 ✂

*Chamaerops*, the only European fan palm, is indigenous in the western Mediterranean, where it can grow to a height of 7 m. The cultivated variety is lower, though it is broad.
This is a low-growing tree with fairly small, fan-shaped leaves on a spiny stem. It has flowerheads consisting of a large number of yellow flowers, and dark yellow fruits, 2-3 cm long. It forms suckers at the base.
*C. humilis* was already a popular plant for growing in tubs in 1593, when it was cultivated in Belgium. It has a brown, fibrous trunk, spiny leaf stems, and yellow clusters of flowers between the leaves. There is often no trunk; *C. humilis* "Macrocarpa" has strikingly large fruits; "Elatior" is larger. This is a slow-growing orangery plant with few requirements. Preferably grow in a special palm pot in well-drained potting compost with loam, leaf-mould and sand. Place in full sunlight in summer and water liberally. The clump should not dry out. Spray plant and feed every 2-4 weeks. In winter, keep in a frost-free, dry spot. Remove brown points, except on the edges. Propagate from seed in early spring, in moist peat in a warm spot. Germination can take a year, and the young plant takes years to become attractive.

# Chrysanthemum

· ⬍ 30-100 ◯ ⚙ 6-10 ▽

*Chrysanthemum* is indigenous in Mediterranean areas and comprises a number of species, one of which is also indigenous in this part of the world: *C. segetum*. In the past, several species, including Ox-eye daisies, were also included in this genus.
This is a herbaceous, usually annual, profusely flowering plant. Many cultivars are cultivated from different parent plants; there are also double or fully double varieties.
*C. carinatum* has bipinnate leaves with pointed lobes and flowerheads, 4-6 cm across, with a dark red heart. The ray flowers of the original species were white with a yellow base; some varieties have coloured rings at the base; "Court Jesters" has ray flowers with beautiful markings; "Poolster" is a large-flowered variety with white flowers and a yellow ring.
*C. coronarium* has bipinnate, light green leaves, flowerheads in panicles 3-5 cm

*Chrysanthemum segetum*
*"Zebra"*

*Chrysanthemum carinatum*
*"Frohe Mischung"*

across, consisting of yellowish-green tube flowers and (dark) yellow ray flowers; "Primrose Gem" and "Golden Gem" have virtually only ray flowers.

*C. multicaule* is a low-growing plant with bluish, spatulate leaves which flowers profusely with golden-yellow flowerheads.

*C. segetum*, corn marigold, has bluish-green, coarsely serrated leaves and flowerheads up to 6 cm across, which are yellow or yellow with a brown heart, such as the "Eastern Star" (syn. "Prado") variety; it flowers only ten weeks after being sown and makes excellent cut flowers.

*C. frutescens*, Marguerite, is a branching sub-shrub, with light green, pinnate, indented leaves, and flowerheads up to 7 cm across, consisting of yellow tube flowers and white ray flowers; take cuttings in autumn in airy soil in a warm spot. Suitable for a spot in full sunlight; repot in nutritious potting compost, and overwinter in a frost-free place. Deadhead flowers regularly. Propagate from seed: in March in a cold frame, end of April outside (except *C. frutescens*), or from cuttings and by dividing plant.

*Chrysanthemum
carinatum
"Dunetii Aurea"*

*Chrysanthemum
coronarium
"Primrose Gem"*

*Cistus altidus*

# Cistus
*Rock rose*

⚘ ↕ up to 180 ○ ❀ 5-8 🪴 🪴

*Cistus* is mainly indigenous in Mediterranean regions, but also in dry, warm regions in Europe, western Asia, North Africa and America. It comprises about 200 species which can easily be crossed, so there are many hybrids. This is an evergreen shrub which is not completely winter-hardy in this part of the world. It has white, pink or yellow flowers, often facing one way, with five thin, slightly crumpled petals and yellow stamens. It flowers for a long time.

*C. crispus* has long, hairy stems and stalkless, lanceolate to oval, very felty, hairy leaves, 2-4 cm long, with a wavy edge, and purplish-red flowers, 4 cm across, on short stalks.
*C. hirsutus* has downy, hairy stems, oval, hairy leaves, 2.5-6 cm long, and white flowers, 4 cm across, with petals stained yellow at the base.
*C. ladanifer* has sticky stems, virtually stalkless, fragrant, lanceolate leaves up to 10 cm long, with sticky grey hairs on the underside, and single, white flowers, 10 cm across, with red blotches at the base.
*C. laurifolius* is (virtually) winter-hardy and up to 2 m tall. It has sticky, hairy stems, aromatic, oval, pointed, dull, dark green leaves 8 cm long, and long-stemmed, white flowers with a yellow heart, approximately 7 cm across, from June to August. There are 2-8 flowers per flowerhead.
*C. x pulverulentus* (*C. albidus* x *C. crispus*) has oblong, greyish-green, wavy leaves, covered with grey hair, and dark cherry-red flowers 6 cm across, e.g., "Sunset".
This plant is suitable for a sunny spot, also in coastal regions. Tolerates sea winds. Grow in a pot in lime-rich soil with some sand, water moderately and feed once a week. Overwinter in a light, frost-free spot to prevent leaves falling, not too warm and not too dry. Deadhead flowers regularly (for a longer flowering period).
Propagate from cuttings in the summer, seed (February to March), and by layering.

*x Citrofortunella microcarpa,*

# x Citrofortunella

⚘ ↕ up to 3 m ↔ up to 1.8 m ◉ ✿
all year round ⚱

x *Citrofortunella*, formerly known as *Citrus microcarpa*, is a cross of the genus *Citrus* and the genus *Fortunella*, probably arising from the species *Fortunella margarita* (kumquat) and *Citrus reticulata*, (tangerine). Only one species is known, x *Citrofortunella microcarpa* (syn. x *C. mitis*), Calamondin. This is a woody-stemmed, evergreen, branching shrub without thorns, and with leathery, shiny green leaves, 5-10 cm long. Orange-like fruits, 4 cm across, develop even on young plants. They are not edible, because of their extremely sour taste, but can be used to make jelly. The fruits require three to four months to develop their colour, and remain on the plant for a long time, up to seven months. The plant flowers up to six times a year with fragrant, white flowers in clusters of three to four.
In summer, this is a suitable plant for a warm, sheltered spot outside, or for inside if it is not too warm (up to 25° C), out of bright sunlight. In the growing season keep moderately moist, feed once a week and pinch out tips occasionally. In winter, it should be kept in a cool place, but not below 8° C, with less water; do not feed. Repot in slightly acid soil, with plenty of leaf-mould or peat and a quarter part clay. Too much lime in the soil causes leaves to turn yellow. It tolerates a few degrees of frost. Propagate from top cuttings in summer at 15-20° C.

# Citrus
*Orange, lemon, tangerine etc.*

🌱 ↕ 1.2-6 m ↔ up to 4 m ◯ ✿ 5-6/8-9 ⚱

*Citrus* comprises about 12 economically important species and a large number of (cultivated) varieties; candied peel also comes from citrus species with a very thick stem; sometimes grapefruit skin is used. *Citrus* wood is yellowish in colour, and is used in marquetry.
This evergreen, spiny shrub or small tree is not winter-hardy. It has oval, often dark green, shiny leaves with oil glands; the white flowers appear in spring to early summer and have five narrow petals.
The fragrant fruits ripen slowly and are rich in vitamin C.

*C. limon*, the lemon tree, has spines up to 2 cm long, and white flowers, followed by lemons, which take a year to ripen and turn yellow.
*C. sinensis*, the orange tree, originates from China. It is a sizeable tree with small spines, sweetly fragrant flowers and delicious fruit up to 10 cm across.
These trees are suitable for a light, warm, sheltered spot out of bright sunlight. Grow in pots in loamy, well-drained, nutritious soil, poor in lime and rich in humus, with some rotted organic manure. Do not plant too deep. Temperature, ideally around 26° C. At lower temperatures (below 14° C) the growth stagnates. Water moderately and feed once a fortnight. Spray only when there are no flowers. Keep in a cool place in winter (4-6° C), and water sparingly, but do not allow to dry out. Prune back weak stems and pinch out tips to promote bushy growth. Rather sensitive to viral infections and insects. Propagate from top cuttings in spring at 28° C in peat with sharp sand. It can also be propagated from seed or by grafting.

*Citrus sinensis*, *Orange*

*Clerodendrum bungei*

## Cordyline

◦ | 1-2(-8) m ↔ 1.8-2.5 m ○ ⊘ ✱ 6 ⊔ ◁

*Cordyline* is indigenous in eastern Asia, Australia, New Zealand and tropical South America, and comprises approximately 15 species. This evergreen, tree-like plant, with or without a trunk, has long leaves ending in a sharp point, and flowers with 60-120 cm long panicles, of small, white flowers.
*C. australis*, New Zealand cabbage plant, is a slow-growing plant, and flowers only after approximately ten years. Sometimes it bears white berries; *C. australis* "Atropurpurea" has partly purple leaves; there are also varieties with red and yellow stripes.
*C. indivisa* has an unbranched trunk, and compact rosettes of thick, leathery leaves, 100-180 cm long, with a long tip. It has pendent clusters of flowers, and takes up a lot of room. *C. indivisa* "Rubra" has red-tinged leaves, 10 cm long.
*C. terminalis* (syn. *C. fruticosa*), Good-luck plant, Ti tree, has a thin, unbranching trunk, lanceolate leaves, 50 cm long, which turn from green to red, and lilac panicles of flowers. It requires high humidity, and does not tolerate bright sunlight. Spray every day. There are a number of varieties with beautifully coloured leaves, such as *C. terminalis* "Firebrand", which has purplish-red leaves with lighter coloured veins; "Madame André", purplish-red leaves; "Tricolor", coloured leaves.
It is suitable for a light spot in full sunlight (except *C. terminalis*). Water liberally during the growing season and feed once a fortnight. It will tolerate a few degrees of frost, but should be overwintered if possible at 10-13° C, fairly dry. Repot only if really necessary, in normal potting compost with coniferous woodland soil. Sensitive to aphids and red spider mite. Propagate from top cuttings (using rooting power), from seed in the spring, and by carefully removing suckers in spring and planting in peat with sand.

## Clerodendrum

⚘ | 2-3 m ↔ 2-3.5 m ○ ✱ 5/7-8/9 ⊔

*Clerodendrum* is mainly indigenous in tropical regions of Africa and Asia, and comprises approximately 400 species, of which only the more or less winter-hardy species from China and Japan are suitable as terrace plants.
This shrub has soft stems which have an unpleasant smell when touched. It has whorls or groups of leaves and terminal clusters of bright coloured, bell-shaped flowers with a long corolla and protruding stamens, and bears berry-like fruits.
*C. bungei* (syn. *C. foetidum*) from China, is a deciduous shrub, not entirely winter-hardy (up to -10° C) and up to 2 m tall, with almost black stems and whorls of long-stemmed, dark green, heart-shaped leaves up to 20 cm long, which emit an unpleasant smell when touched. It has lilac-pink, fragrant flowers in large, striking clusters, and forms suckers.
*C. trichotomum*, from China and Japan, grows to 6 m tall in its natural habitat. It is a deciduous, moderately winter-hardy shrub with oval, foul-smelling leaves up to 22 cm long, downy on the underside, and fragrant, star-shaped, white flowers with a red calyx in large clusters, 15-22 cm long. It has small, bright blue to black fruits; the *fargesii* variety is more winter-hardy, with less downy, bright green leaves; the young stems and leaves are purplish.
This plant requires a sheltered, well-drained spot. Grow it in a pot in nutritious soil. Propagate from root cuttings (using rooting powder in a warm place), from suckers and by dividing the plant.

## Crinodendron

⚘ | 3-4 m ↔ up to 2 m ⊘ ✱ 5-8 ⊔ ◁

*Crinodendron* is indigenous in temperate regions of South America and comprises two species. The name is derived from the Greek words "krinon" (lily) and "dendron" (tree), which refer to the growth and flowers of this tree. It is a small,

*Cordyline australis*

*Crinodendron patagua*

evergreen tree with spreading leaves, and single, pendent flowers with a bell-shaped calyx and five serrated or lobed petals hanging from thick stems in the leaf axilla.
*C. hookerianum* (syn. *C. lanceolata*), the lantern tree, is much lower when it is cultivated than in its natural habitat. It has stiff, pointed, serrated leaves, 4-12 cm long, which are shiny green on the upper side, and numerous, lantern-like, fleshy, coral-red flowers, 3-4 cm long, hanging from one-year-old shoots.
*C. patagua* (syn. *C. dependens*) is a more vigorous shrub with oval leaves, 8 cm long, with a serrated leaf margin, and bell-shaped, white flowers, approximately 2 cm long.
It is suitable for a sheltered spot in moist potting compost, preferably slightly acid (and poor in lime). Keep clump moist at all times, but ensure that it is well drained. Spray regularly, and feed once a fortnight during the growing period. It is sensitive to various scale insects; combat this by dabbing with meths. After a few days, sponge with meths and soap; repeat a few times. Propagate from cuttings of strong young shoots in August/September. Let these take root in a moist mixture of leaf-mould and peat.

top: Crinum x powellii 'Album'
bottem: Crinum x powellii

# Crinum

⬡ ↕ 30-120 ↔ 40-100 ○ ❁ 7-8 ! ⊔

*Crinum*, indigenous in warm and tropical regions all over the world, comprises about 100 species. These are often evergreen, sometimes with enormous bulbs which develop upwards in a bottle shape. It has unstemmed, strap-shaped or sword-shaped leaves, and lily-like flowers, 8-10 cm long, in terminal umbels with a few basal leaves on long, bare stems; after fertilization, large seeds develop, which germinate *in situ*, forming a new bulb.

*C. x powellii* and *C. moorei*, from southern Africa, are the most cultivated species. The fragrant pink to pinkish-red flowers with a slightly arching corolla, grow on the leafless flower stem, 70-140 cm long, at the same time that the leaves appear on the plant. The bulbs of *C. moorei* grow 15-20 cm in diameter, and have a thick neck up to 35 cm long; *C. moorei* "Album" has white flowers. *C. x powellii* is a profusely-flowering cross of *C. bulbispermum* and *C. moorei*. It will tolerate a few degrees of frost, and has reddish to white flowers; *C. x powellii* "Album" has white flowers; "Krelagel", deep pink; "Haarlemse", pink. Plant in a shallow hollow (with the tip protruding above the ground) in nutritious soil, water regularly and feed once a month. Overwinter in a cool place, not below 5° C. Water less and do not feed. The flowers are also good for cutting. Propagate from seed and by removing offsets; seeds which have germinated can be potted and cultivated.

# Echium

○ ↕ 40-200 ○ ❁ 6-9 ⊔ ⊔

*Echium* comprises many species, including *Echium vulgare*, Viper's bugloss, which is indigenous in this part of the world. The scientific name is derived from the Greek word, "echis" (viper). The flowers are rich in nectar and therefore attract many bees and other insects.
These herbaceous annuals, biennials or perennials have striking flowers arranged in two rows next to each other, facing alternately to the left and right. Many annual and biennial species are suitable for growing in the garden.

*E. fastuosum*, from the Canary Islands, is a
shrub-like, evergreen perennial, with soft,
greyish-green or white hairy leaves, and
numerous flowers in large, compact,
cone-shaped clusters.
Suitable for a sunny spot, especially in poor,
lime-rich, sandy soil. Feed once a month.
Overwinter in a sunny spot, not below 5° C
at night, but warmer in the daytime.
The clump should be kept fairly dry. It can
be repotted in spring, taking care not to
damage the taproot.
Propagate from seed.

# Eriobotrya
*Loquat*

[icons] up to 2.5 m rarely

*Eriobotrya* is indigenous in subtropical
China and Japan, and comprises 30 species.
They are evergreen shrubs or small trees
which produce large quantities of
plum-shaped fruits in warm regions.
These are used to make jelly and desserts.
Only one species is cultivated.
*E. japonica*, Loquat, has shiny green,
leathery leaves, 20-30 cm long, with deep
veins; the underside is covered with brown
hairs, the young leaves are covered with
soft, silvery hairs. The plant rarely flowers
in this part of the world.
It is suitable for a sheltered, slightly shady
or sunny spot. Feed once a fortnight.
Overwinter at 5-10° C, and keep fairly dry.
Repot young plants once a year, older
plants every three to five years, in a mixture
of two parts potting compost to one part
clay. Prune only when the plant grows too
large. Propagate from seed, using the pips of
the fruit, in moist peat.

top: *Echium fastuosum*

*Eriobotrya japonica*, Loquat

*Erythrina crista-galli*
*Coral tree*

# Erythrina
*Coral tree*

🌱 ⬍ 1-2 m ⬌ up to 2 m ○ ❀ 6-9 ! 🪴

The name *Erythrina* is derived from the
Greek word "erythros" (red). This plant is
indigenous in all (sub)tropical regions and
comprises about 100 species.
It is usually a shrub or small tree with
hook-shaped, spiny leaves in groups of
three, and characteristic large, red or orange,
pea-like flowers in racemes up to 50 cm
long. The pods between the seeds are
indented to a greater or lesser extent.
*E. crista-galli*, Cockspur coral-tree, has oval,
sea-green leaves up to 10 cm long, and
waxy flowers on reddish twigs. When they
have finished flowering, the shoots die off.
Prune back to the old wood. *E. crista-galli*
"Compacta" has a more compact growth
and flowers as a very young plant.
Propagate from cuttings.
*E. humeana*, the coral tree from Natal, South
Africa, is up to 4 m tall and semi-evergreen.
It has dark red flowers which protrude
above the leaves, like the horse chestnut.

It flowers as a very young plant.
It is suitable for a warm, sheltered spot in
full sunlight. Water regularly and apply a
liquid feed once a week. Water less and do
not feed when it has flowered. Overwinter
at approximately 5° C, almost dry; the
leaves drop off. In spring, prune back to
15 cm from the base, and gradually give
more water. Harden off carefully. Repot
older plants every five years, young plants
every year, in well-drained, nutritious soil in
potting compost with extra clay and sand.
Propagate from seed (it takes years for the
plant to flower), by dividing the plant and
from cuttings in spring at 25° C.

# Eucalyptus
*Gum tree*

🌴 ⬍ up to 8 m ⬌ up to 3 m ○ ❀ 5-8 🪴

*Eucalyptus* is indigenous particularly in
Australia and Tasmania. There are a few
species in the east of Indonesia and
Malaysia. The genus comprises more than
500 species. It is a very old genus, and

fossils have been found from the Eocene period, 54 million years ago.

Usually they are evergreen trees which bear different types of (aromatic) leaves at different stages; in many species the young plants have unstemmed whorls of broad leaves, while the mature trees have narrow, spreading leaves on stems. Because of the hanging foliage, the tree provides very little shade. Many species have striking bark. The buds are angular with a cover which falls off when the flower opens; it is actually part of the petals. The flowers have colourful stamens, and the large quantity of nectar on the receptacle attracts many birds and beetles which pollinate the tree. The flowers usually grow in small umbels; after flowering, there are capsules.

*E. gunnii*, cider gum, is almost winter-hardy, with bluish-white stems, bluish-green, young leaves and long, hanging, green older leaves. It flowers after five to six years when the tree is 5 m tall, with white flowers.

*E. pauciflora*, White Sally, is almost winter-hardy, especially *E. pauciflora* subsp. *debeuzevillei*, which often has several curved trunks and a flaky, white and grey marbled bark. The variety *nana* is like a shrub, up to 6 m tall, with narrower leaves.

*E. niphophila*, Snow gum, is virtually winter-hardy with a decorative bark, which is white and blue in young trees. After four to five years it flakes and the lower bark is grey or brown. The leaves are bluish-green to orange and it has white clusters of flowers in summer.

Suitable for a spot in full sunlight, sheltered against cold wind, in any fertile, well-drained soil. It is resistant to drought, but grows better in moist soil. The temperature should not fall below 10° C at night, and reach at least 15° C in the day. Overwinter at at least 5° C. The plants can be pruned to keep them smaller with young leaves. Propagate by sowing seeds from capsules.

# Euryops

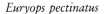 | 50-70 ↔ up to 1.2 m ○ ✿ 5 🍶

*Euryops* is indigenous from southern Africa to Saudi Arabia and comprises about 70 species.

This is an evergreen shrub with lobed or pinnate leaves. It has yellow, daisy-like flowerheads with a heart consisting of serrated tube flowers, surrounded by spreading ray flowers, which grow on leafless stems in the leaf axilla or terminally.

*E. acraeus* (erroneously *E. evansii*) has compact grey stems, narrow, silvery leaves up to 2.5 cm long in groups, and white flowerheads with about eleven ray flowers,

2.5 cm across. Preferably plant in soil with a lot of grit.

*E. pectinatus* has felty, grey or white, hairy leaves with serrated lobes, and canary yellow flowerheads 4-5 cm across, with 13-20 ray flowers on stems up to 15 cm long.

Suitable for a spot in full sunlight at about 20° C in normal, well-drained potting compost with some clay and old cow manure. Water liberally, and do not allow temperature to fall below 5° C at night during the resting period. Deadhead regularly, and prune into shape in spring. Can easily be propagated from cuttings and from seed.

*Eucalyptus camalduleusis,*
*Gum tree*

*Euryops pectinatus*

*Fatsia japonica*

# Felicia

⬚ ○ ↕ 10-45 ○ ✿ 6-8 🍷

*Felicia* is indigenous in particular in South Africa. It comprises 60 species and is very similar to *Aster*.
The leaves grow in whorls or in pairs; the long-stemmed flowerheads have yellow, androgynous tube flowers, surrounded by two rings of usually blue, female ray flowers; there are also white and mauve varieties. In dull weather the flowers remain closed.
*F. ameiloides* (syn. *F. capensis, Agathaea coelestis*), blue marguerite, is a perennial with whorls of bright green, round to oval leaves and sky-blue flowers up to 3 cm across; the cultivars include "White", with white ray flowers.
*F. amoena* (syn. *F. pappei, Aster pappei*) is up to 20 cm tall, with fleshy leaves and porcelain blue ray flowers.
*F. bergeriana* (syn. *Aster bergerianus*), Kingfisher daisy, is a branching annual up to 20 cm tall. It has hairy, oval, lanceolate, serrated leaves 2-4 cm long, yellow and black tube flowers and bright blue ray flowers.
*F. tenella* (syn. *F. fragilis*) is very hairy,

# Fatsia

⬚ ↕ 1.8 m or more ↔ 1.2-1.8 m ◉ ✿ 9-10 ⬚

*Fatsia japonica* (syn. *Aralia sieboldii*) is indigenous in Japan, Korea and Taiwan. It is the only species in this genus, and was imported to western Europe at the end of the 19th century.
This strong shrub does not spread much, and has rust-coloured, hairy stems, attractive, leathery, palmate, indented, shiny leaves up to 40 cm wide, and white flowers in terminal clusters; the fruits are fairly large, fleshy berries. *F. japonica* "Variegata" has leaves with a white margin.
This plant is suitable for a shady spot that is not too warm.
It tolerates sea wind and light to heavy shade very well. Water generously in warm weather and feed with liquid manure once a month during the growing season. Overwinter frost-free. Propagate from seed under glass in spring, or from summer cuttings.

*middle: Felicia bergeriana*

10-20 cm tall, with narrow, straight leaves up to 5 cm long, and violet-blue ray flowers. This plant is suitable for a very sunny, sheltered spot. Protect from (too much) rain. It requires well-drained, nutritious soil and a pot with a diameter of at least 12 cm. Apply liquid feed once a fortnight. Temperature in winter should not fall below 7° C. Before repotting in spring, prune back hard. Propagate from seed at the beginning of May, or from cuttings for perennials in June/August in moist peat. When they have taken root, put them in pots in threes. Pinch out the tips when the plant is 6-7 cm tall for bushy growth.

# Ficus
*Fig*

🌳 ↕ 1.5-4.5(-9) m ↔ 3-5 m ○ ✿ 5 ⬚

*Ficus* is indigenous in tropical and subtropical regions, and comprises more than 800 species, of which *F. carica* is often cultivated in Mediterranean regions, both for its dense, shady crown and for its fruit. Many species are well-known house plants in this part of the world.

This climbing or creeping tree or shrub is related to the mulberry. It is usually evergreen, and often contains a milky juice. It forms fleshy fruit, figs, from a hollow receptacle. In dioecious species (separate male and female plants) insects are responsible for pollination.
There is a special sort of gall wasp for every species of *Ficus*.
*F. carica*, the common fig, is a shrub-like tree with a rounded crown. It sometimes grows wild in sheltered spots, e.g., on humid city walls. It has palmate, indented leaves up to 20 cm long and wide, and yellowish-green flowers. Only the female tree bears the tasty seed or common figs; the fruits appear on the young wood in the leaf axilla and can be harvested several times a year in hot summers. When the leaves drop off in winter, the young figs remain until the following season. There are many cultivars which tolerate light or moderate frost.
Suitable for a light spot out of very bright sunlight; the young figs often drop off if it is very dry, if there are great fluctuations in temperature, or little sunlight. Plants in tubs should be overwintered in a frost-free, well-ventilated place at 0-5° C; prune back in winter to 4-6 leaves, in the second year, to 40 cm. Repot in spring every 3-5 years in fertile, sandy soil, with one third part clay or loam, and a generous quantity of rotted cow manure. Propagate from winter cuttings and by layering. The milky juice can cause skin irritations.

*Ficus carica*

*Fortunella margarita,*
*Kumquat*

# Fortunella
*Kumquat*

🌱 ↕ 1-4 m ↔ 1-2.5 m ○ ❁ 4-6 ✤

*Fortunella* is indigenous in eastern Asia and the Malaysian archipelago. It comprises 6 species, and was named after the British botanist, Robert Fortune, who imported *Fortunella* to Europe in the nineteenth century. This is a small, evergreen tree, closely related to *Citrus*, but with smaller fruit and a hollow flower stem. Sometimes it has spiny branches. The long-stemmed, thick, blunt, shiny leaves have a rounded margin and look spotted, because of the large number of glands on the upper side. The fragrant white flowers grow singly or in small groups. The edible fruits resemble very small, elongated oranges. They are actually orange, sweet, spicy or sour-tasting berries containing many pips. Eat fresh, or use for marmalade and fruit compote.
*F. margarita*, Nagami kumquat, is 3-4 m tall. The branches have few or no thorns, and the lanceolate, short-stemmed leaves are 6-10 cm long. The flowers are 1 cm across, and the round or oblong, orangey-yellow, sour fruits are 2-4 cm long.
*F. japonica*, Marumi kumquat, is a low, bushy shrub, sometimes with spines and broader leaves than the previous species. It has round, bright orange, sweet fruits. It requires a sunny spot. Water regularly, overwinter in a frost-free place, minimum 5° C, and keep drier, but the leaves should not drop off. Prune back in spring, and repot in a mixture of two parts of the red clay in which it is sold, with two parts of leaf-mould and one part of rotted cow manure. Watch out for yellow leaves which result from chlorosis (iron deficiency). Water with chelated iron occasionally (several grammes to 1 litre of water; alternatively, water in which some rusty nails have been soaked will also suffice). Propagate from seed; cuttings or grafting works better.

32

# Fremontodendron
*Flannel flower*

🌿 ↕ 3-4.5 m ↔ up to 3 m ○ ✿ 5-9 🪣

*Fremontodendron* is indigenous in California and Mexico, and comprises four to six species. It is a vigorous, branching shrub; the branches are covered with hair. It has spreading, three to five-lobed, usually dull green, sometimes lighter leaves, and large, yellow, star-shaped flowers with a five-lobed calyx like a crown, and five spreading stamens in a star shape on the young runners. After flowering, it develops hard, bristly capsules.
*F. californicum* (syn. *Fremontia californica*) is a very hairy, semi-evergreen, which flowers profusely; it has fairly thick, round leaves with three lobes, which are hairy on the underside, and bright yellow flowers, 3-5 cm across, with a flat, spreading calyx; there are several varieties which are sometimes classified as separate species.
*F. mexicanum* has hairy stems with hairy, deeply indented leaves up to 14 cm long, and orangey-yellow, saucer-shaped flowers, 5-8 cm across, concealed amongst the foliage.
*Fremontodendron* "California Glory", a cross of *F. californicum* and *F. mexicanum*, is a fast-growing shrub which flowers profusely, with dark yellow flowers, 10 cm across. It is a beautiful shrub, but unfortunately does not live long.
Suitable for a spot in full sunlight, as a tub plant, or for training (taller). Fill the pot with well-drained soil consisting of equal parts of leaf-mould, clay and well-rotted cow manure. Keep moderately moist and feed regularly with organic manure. Overwinter in a frost-free place, keep fairly dry. Prune back after flowering to retain shape. Propagate from seed in early spring, and from cuttings of young runners in summer, which take root at 20° C.

*Fremontodendron Californicum*

*Fremontodendron "California Glory"*

*Fuchsia hybrid*

# Fuchsia

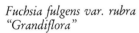 ⬇ 50-150 ↔ up to 100 ○ ◉ ✿ 5-10 ❀

*Fuchsia* is indigenous particularly in Central and South America, but also in New Zealand (the Maoris used the juice to decorate their bodies) and on Tahiti. It comprises about 100 species. The first *Fuchsia* species were not cultivated in Europe until 1788; by about 1825, the first crosses had appeared. The plants became very popular because of the striking, prolific flowers.

This shrub-like plant has flowers with a long corolla ending in four sepals and four overlapping petals, four long and four short stamens, and a long pistil; often the calyx and crown have different colours. The fruits are edible berries. There are also double cultivars.

*F. arborescens*, the tree fuchsia, has dark

*Fuchsia fulgens var. rubra "Grandiflora"*

green, smooth-edged leaves and fragrant, small, erect flowers in clusters, with a lavender corolla coloured crown and a red calyx.

*F. boliviana* has hairy shoots, whorls of oval leaves up to 15 cm long, and hanging flowers in clusters with a red calyx; "Luxurians" has a pinky-white calyx.

*F. coccinea* has hairy stems, oval, serrated leaves with red veins, in whorls or groups of three, and flowers with a short tube, red calyx and violet corolla. *F. denticulata* is 1.5-4 m tall, with red stems, and lanceolate, serrated leaves with red veins in groups of three or four. The flowers have a fairly long tube, and hang on thin stalks; they have a pink or pale red calyx and an orange to purplish-red crown.

*F. excorticata* is a broad shrub, with a flaky, light brown bark, spreading oval to lanceolate, dark green leaves, and flowers with a green calyx at first, later turning purplish-red, and a dark purple corolla. The almost black fruits are 1 cm in diameter. *F. fuchsia* has thick roots, hairy, reddish stems, whorls of hairy, greyish-green, heart-shaped leaves, and flowers in clusters with a long, narrow tube, stamens out of sight, and a pale red calyx with a bright red corolla.

*F. magellanica*, Ladies' Eardrops, is a virtually winter-hardy, attractive shrub which grows up to 1-1.5 m tall in this part

of the world. It has whorls of serrated leaves and flowers which grow singly or in groups in the leaf axilla, usually with a red calyx and purple corolla. There are many cultivars, such as "Macrostemma", with large leaves, and "Molinea", with lilac-pink flowers.

*F. procumbens* is a creeping shrub with very small, heart-shaped, dark green leaves, erect flowers with a green calyx with a red point, and no petals. The light red berries have a silvery tinge and grow up to 2 cm in diameter. Cultivate as a hanging plant, do not remove dead flowers.

There are many hundreds of cultivars; most are crosses of *F. fulgens* and *F. magellanica*, usually described as *F. x hybrida*. They have heavy, usually hanging flowers, and there are selections in every shape and colour; hanging, shrub-like or like a small tree. Suitable for any light spot with some shade, also indoors. Overwinter in a frost-free, cool, fairly dry spot, minimum 3° C at night, e.g., in a shed. It is deciduous and can therefore be kept in the dark in winter. Water less from September. It can be pruned before or after the resting period in winter; prune back main stems to two or three eyes. Repot in early spring in potting compost with some manure. Place in a lighter, warmer spot, and pinch out the tips regularly (always remove the third pair of leaves) up to the beginning of May. In the

second half of the season, feed once a week. Remove dead flowers. Propagate from cuttings in an airy mixture of peat and sharp sand, using young (not woody) shoots with three to four pairs of leaves. Botanical species can also be propagated from seed.

*Gerbera jamesonii*

# Gerbera

◯ ⬍ up to 45 ⬌ 40-60 ◯ ⚙ 6 ⚒ 🪴 🪴

*Gerbera* is indigenous in Asia, Africa and Madagascar. It comprises 70 species, and has been cultivated since the 18th century; they are popular cut flowers.

This is a perennial, herbaceous plant with long-stemmed, undivided or four-lobed, often hairy leaves which grow in a rosette from the roots. The flowerheads grow on long, leafless stalks with androgynous tube flowers surrounded by a single or double ring of ray flowers.

*G. jamesonii* hybrids from South Africa form the basis of modern gerbera, with flowers in every shade of pink, red, orange, yellow or white. It is a very hairy plant with large, lobed leaves up to 20 cm broad and 30 cm long, with single flowerheads varying from 12-16 cm in diameter. There are also cultivars with differently coloured hearts or double flowers.

This plant is suitable for a sunny, warm spot; it can also be placed on a light windowsill. Water liberally in summer, and apply liquid feed once a fortnight. Overwinter in a frost-free place, minimum 5° C. Keep moderately moist and remove old leaves. Repot in early May in pots 12-20 cm in diameter in nutritious soil, e.g., equal parts of clay, leaf-mould and cow manure. For cut flowers, change the water regularly and cut the stalks. Propagate by dividing plants every 3 to 4 years, and from seed.

*middle:*
*Fuchsia magellanica*
*"Gracillis"*

*middle:*
*Halimiocystus ocymoides*

# x Halimiocystus

🌿 ↕ 30-60 ↔ 30-100 ○ ❁ 5-9 🍶

x *Halimiocystus*, is a cross of the genus
*Halimium* and the genus *Cistus*, which both
belong to the same family. Its characteristics
are somewhere between those of the two
parent plants. It is a woody-stemmed,
evergreen plant which is found in
Mediterranean areas, but also further north.
x *H.* "Ingwersenii" from Portugal, is a
natural cross, probably of *Halimium
umbellatum* and *Cistus hirsutus*. It flowers for
a long time and has white, woolly, hairy
shoots, narrow, dark green, lanceolate leaves
up to 30 cm long, and white flowers about
2 cm across with white, hairy sepals.
x *H. sahucii*, a cross of *Halimium
umbellatum* and *Cistus salviifolius*, has more
or less horizontal stems, oblong to
lanceolate, hairy leaves, 3 cm long, and 2-5
white flowers up to 3 cm in diameter.
x *H. wintonensis*, a hybrid of *Halimium
lasianthum* and *Cistus salviifolius*, is
cultivated in England, and has oval to
lanceolate, hairy, greyish-green leaves,
2-5 cm long, and white with yellow flowers
up to 5 cm in diameter, with a red ring in
the heart. x *H. wintonensis* "Merristwood
Cream" has cream flowers.
This shrub is suitable for a very sunny,
warm, sheltered spot. It requires a lot of
water in summer, sometimes twice a day in
warm weather, and should be fed once a
week. Overwinter in a light, cool place,
minimum 5° C. Keep fairly dry, but do not
allow to dry out. Repot young plants every
spring, older plants every 2 to 3 years, in
potting compost with clay. Propagate from
cuttings of young shoots with a heel in peat
and sand. Layering also works well, but can
take two years.

*x Halimiocystus sahucii*

# Halimium

🌿 ↕ 50-100 ↔ 60-120 ○ ❁ 5-6 🍶

*Halimium* is indigenous in Mediterranean
regions. It comprises 14 species and
resembles *Helianthemum*, the rock rose,
though the flowers of the latter have a pistil
with a longer curved style.
This is an evergreen, creeping, often hairy
(sub-)shrub with leaves in whorls, delicate
yellow, red or purple flowers with many
stamens and a pistil with a short, straight
style, 3-5 sepals and five petals.
After flowering, capsules appear which
spring open to reveal the seeds.
*H. halimifolium* is a branching, hairy shrub
with peeling stems, short-stemmed leaves
covered with grey hair, and bright yellow
terminal flowers up to 4 cm in diameter, in

# Heliotropium
*Heliotrope*

• ⚘ ↕ 0.3-1.6 m ↔ 30-45 ○ ✿ 5-9 ▯

*Heliotropium* is indigenous in subtropical regions of the northern hemisphere.
It comprises about 250 species. Only one species is widely cultivated.
These are usually annual or perennial herbaceous plants with spreading, oval leaves with deep veins, and vanilla-scented, lilac to deep purple flowers, tightly packed in an umbel-like scorpioid cyme with five fused petals at the base. There are many hybrids differing in height, the size of the flowers, the colour and compactness of the flowers and leaves, but often these are not scented.
*H. arborescens* (syn. *H. peruvianum*) is a (sub-)shrub from Peru, where it can grow up to 50 years old and up to 2 m tall. It has been cultivated here since 1740 and was widely used in the past for the flowerbeds of stately homes. It is not winter-hardy in this part of the world, and is often grown as an annual; cultivars include "Marine", 40-60 m tall, dark leaves, large, deep violet flowers; "Early Violet", up to 45 cm tall, fragrant, violet-blue flowers.
This plant is suitable for a sunny spot; it requires a lot of water, but does not tolerate much rain. Feed occasionally. Overwinter in a light, cool place, minimum 12° C. Keep moderately moist. Repot every year in nutritious, lime-rich, well-drained soil. Propagate from seed in March at approximately 18° C, and from top cuttings in January or August at 20° C. Pinch out tips regularly or cultivate as a small tree. During the flowering period they attract many insects, butterflies and bumblebees.

loose clusters on straight stems. The petals have a black eye.
*H. lasianthum* subsp. *formosum* (syn. *H. formosum*) from Portugal, is a broad, spreading shrub with woolly, hairy, short-stemmed leaves with 3 clear veins, golden-yellow flowers, 4 cm across, with central, purplish-brown blotches; "Concolor" has unblotched, golden-yellow flowers.
*H. ocymoides* (syn. *Helianthemum ocymoides*, *Cistus algarvensis*) is a compact, spreading, white, hairy shrub, less tall than other species. The non-flowering stems have grey, hairy, stemmed leaves; the flowering stems have green, unstemmed leaves and large, warm yellow flowers, 2 cm across, in big, loose clusters. The petals are blotched with chestnut-brown spots.
This is suitable for a very sunny, sheltered spot and is resistant to cold, though not in combination with a lot of rain. Overwinter in a frost-free place and repot in well-drained soil which is not too heavy. Propagate from summer cuttings, 5-8 cm long, in a mixture of peat and sharp sand. They form roots at 12-16° C; plants can also be propagated from seed.

*Heliotropium arborescens hybrid, Heliotrope*

*Hibiscus rosa-sinensis,*
*Chinese rose*

# Hibiscus
*Chinese rose*

🌿 ⬍ 1-2 m ↔ 0.8-1.2 m ◯ ✺ 8-10 ⬛

*Hibiscus* is found almost everywhere in the world and comprises approximately 300 species. The genus includes all sorts of annual and perennial herbaceous plants, shrubs and trees.
The young shoots are usually hairy with whorls of palmate, lobed leaves, and white, pink, red, purple or yellow flowers in the top leaf axilla, sometimes growing singly,

*Hibiscus paramutabilis*

sometimes in groups, usually with a bell-shaped, five-lobed calyx and five petals. The stamens are fused in a tube shape. There are also cultivars with double or semi-double flowers.
*H. moscheutos* has serrated, lanceolate-oval, unlobed leaves with white hair on the underside, and white, cream, pink or red flowers, often with a red or purple heart; it requires lime-rich, loamy soil.
*H. rosa-sinensis*, Chinese rose, the best known species, is a profusely flowering shrub with long-stemmed, oval leaves, 5-15 cm long and 2.5 cm wide, single flowers up to 20 cm across in the leaf axilla with an extra calyx with 7-10 sepals, originally red, though there are now varieties with single and double flowers in lilac, dark red, salmon, yellow and white.
*H. rosa-sinensis* "Cooperi" has small, blotched leaves and small red flowers; "Variegata" has coloured leaves.
*H. schizopetalus* is a shrub with thin, hanging stems, short-stemmed leaves, and elegant, long-stemmed red flowers, approximately 7 cm across, with fringed, indented petals and short, protruding stamens and pistil curving upwards.
It prefers temperatures from 15-20° C.
*H. syriacus* is a winter-hardy, broad, spreading shrub with pink, red, purple or blue flowers. *H. syriacus* "Bluebird", bluish-purple; "Duc de Brabant", double, deep purple flowers; "Snowdrift", white flowers. This plant is suitable for a light, sunny spot. Protect against bright sunlight and water liberally in warm weather. Apply liquid feed once a month during the growing season. Water regularly in winter, and do not allow temperature to drop below 15° C to ensure the plants keep flowering. Repot annually in March in pots 20-30 cm in diameter in equal parts of leaf-mould, clay and old cow manure. Prune back at the same time. Propagate from summer cuttings in July, using 8-10 cm long top cuttings of non-flowering shoots in moist peat at 18-20° C. Pinch out tips several times. It is also possible to propagate plants from seed.

# Hosta
*Plantain lily*

◉ ⬍ 40-100 ↔ 30-100 ◓ ◉ ✺ 6-9 ❋

*Hosta* is indigenous in eastern Asia, especially in Japan, and comprises about 25-30 species. It is widely cultivated as a garden plant and now grows all over the world. This is a herbaceous, perennial plant with a sturdy, short, branching rhizome, broad

leaves in rosettes, often with colourful markings and deep veins, and flowering stems with small bracts and terminal clusters of hanging, bell-shaped flowers. *Hosta albo-marginata* (syn. *H. sieboldii, H. lancifolia* "Albomarginata") has leaves up to 15 cm long with a (yellowish) white margin, and flowering stems up to 90 cm tall, with 20-30 violet flowers, 5 cm long, with yellow stamens; "Alba" has white flowers.
*H. x fortunei* (syn. *H. sieboldiana* "Fortunei") is a strong cross with grooved, winged leaf stalks with greyish-green leaves up to 12 cm long, and flowering stems up to 60 cm tall with tube-shaped, pale violet flowers, 3.5 cm long, with bluish-purple stamens. "Marginata Alba" has white leaf margins.
*H. sieboldiana* "Glauca" (syn. *H. glauca*) has strong, bluish-green leaves, 30-40 cm long, with beautiful veined markings when mature. In the autumn they turn yellow. The flowering stems are up to 75 cm tall with white flowers, 5 cm long, in June.
*H. ventricosa* (syn. *H. coerulea, H. ovata*) is a compact plant with dark green, shiny, oval leaves, and flowering stems up to 90 cm tall, with deep purple flowers; "Variegata" has coloured leaves.
This plant is suitable for a light, shady spot. It requires normal potting compost with some organic manure. Propagate by dividing plant and from seed in spring. Sensitive to slugs.

*Hosta elata*

*Iochroma coccinea*

# Iochroma

⚘ ↕ 1.5-2 m ○ 🌱

*Iochroma* is indigenous in Central America, e.g., Brazil, and comprises 25 species.
It is a shrub or small tree, usually more or less hairy, with whorls or rosettes of smooth-edged, undivided leaves, and white, yellow, red or purple flowers in clusters or in pairs, with a five-lobed calyx and a long corolla ending in five lobes.
*I. coccinea* is covered in downy hair and has oval-lanceolate leaves, 8-12 cm long, with a sharp point, and clusters of bright red flowers, 4-5 cm long, with a yellow throat.
*I. cyanea* has greyish leaves up to 15 cm long and pendent, terminal clusters of lavender to purple flowers, 4-8 cm long.
This plant is suitable for a warm, sunny spot. Occasionally add plant food to the water. Prune only to retain shape in spring. In winter do not allow the temperature to fall below 5° C, and water less. Repot in spring in fairly fertile, well-drained soil which should not dry out. Propagate from seed and cuttings in moist peat.

*Isomeris arborea*

a strong smell when touched. The flowers grow in large, branching clusters and have a small calyx with four sepals, yellow petals, six protruding stamens and one pistil; the ovary develops into a swollen, hanging capsule in two parts.
This plant is suitable for a sunny spot. Overwinter in a cool, frost-free place at approximately 5° C.
Propagate from seed.

# Isomeris

○ ↕ -100 ✿ 2-5 ⬚

*Isomeris arborea*, the only species in this genus, is indigenous in California and Mexico, and belongs to the same family as *Cleome*, the spider flower.
This is a woody-stemmed plant with spreading leaves, 1-3.5 cm long, which emit

# Jasminum
*Jasmine*

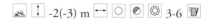 -2(-3) m ↔ ○ ⦸ ✿ 3-6 ⬚

*Jasminum* is indigenous in tropical and subtropical regions in Asia, and comprises 300 species.
This is a woody-stemmed plant, usually with climbing or twining, mostly green stems, and often fragrant flowers. The petals are partly fused in a tube-shaped corolla. They flower on one-year-old wood.
*J. mesnyi* (syn. *J. primulinum*), primrose jasmine, from western China, has green, angular, hanging stems, shiny, dark green leaves up to 7 cm long, divided into three leaflets, and bright yellow flowers up to 3 cm across. It resembles winter jasmine, *J. nudiflorum*, but flowers in March/April.
*J. officinale*, common jasmine, has pinnate leaves, 7-12 cm long, with an extra long, pointed, top leaf, and fragrant white flowers about 2.5 cm long, in clusters of 3-10 together; "Aureovariegatum" has coloured yellow leaves and white flowers; "Grandiflorum" has larger flowers with a pinkish tinge.
This plant is suitable for a light spot, or in full sunlight. It requires some support. Water regularly and feed once a fortnight. Prune back hard after flowering. Pinch out tips of young plants regularly for good branching growth. Overwinter in a light spot at 2-8° C, no bright sunlight, little water. Repot every other year in early spring in a mixture of (beech) leaf-mould with clay or loam, sand and old cow manure. Propagate from cuttings at 20° C in a mixture of peat and sand; from seed, by removing shoots with roots, and by layering.

*Jasminum mesnyi,*
*Primrose jasmine*

# Kochia

• ‖ 60-150 ↔ 30-60 ○ ▽

*Kochia* is indigenous in temperate and
tropical regions of the Old World.
It comprises about 90 species.
This is usually an annual, herbaceous plant
which grows very quickly. It has pale or
bright green, very narrow leaves, and
unremarkable flowerheads with greenish
flowers which grow singly or in clusters.
*K. scoparia*, burning bush or summer
cypress, from southeast Europe, is a bushy,
spherical shrub. It is cultivated particularly
for its foliage and has insignificant, small
green flowers; "Acapulco Silver", silvery;
"Tricophylla", pale green, turning reddish in
autumn.
This plant does well in full sunlight and
tolerates wind. It requires nutritious soil.
Water regularly, especially in warm weather.
Apply liquid manure once a fortnight when
the plants are 20 cm tall, or more.
Propagate from seed in March, under glass,
or in April/May.

*Kochia scoparia "Acapulco Silver"*

# Kunzea

≋ ‖ 1-2.5 m ○ ▽

*Kunzea* is indigenous in Australia and
comprises 30 species.
This is an evergreen shrub, usually with
spreading, very small, smooth-edged leaves,
small, unstemmed flowers with a five-lobed
calyx fused with the capsule, and five
spreading petals with many long stamens
and a long pistil.
*K. ambigua* (syn. *K. corifolia*) has pointed,
oblong-lanceolate leaves, 1.5 cm long, and
terminal, unstemmed, whitish flowers with
more than 30 stamens, half as long again as
the corolla, growing in leafy, short or long,
bottle brush-like spikes.
*K. ericifolia* grows to a height of 4.5 m in its
natural habitat. The stems end in terminal,
yellow, spherical flowerheads, 1.5-2 cm
across, forming a dense hedge.
This plant is suitable for a sunny spot.
It requires acid soil, rich in humus, with
some clay. Prune back hard. Propagate from
seed and cuttings.

*Kunzea ambigua*

*Lagerstroemia indica*

# Lagerstroemia

⟨icons⟩ ↕ 1-6 m ↔ -2 m ○ ✲ 7-10 🛆

*Lagerstroemia* is indigenous in tropical regions in Asia and Australia, and comprises approximately 50 species.
This is a shrub-like, deciduous plant with whorls of simple, shiny leaves, and striking flowers with six petals, often with fringed or frizzy edges and a large number of stamens. After flowering, there are 3-6 capsules with flaps with winged seeds.
*L. indica*, Crape myrtle, from China and Korea is a tree with several trunks.
It flowers profusely on the young, brownish-red, squarish shoots.
The unstemmed or short-stemmed, smooth-edged, oval leaves, 3-6 cm long, turn yellow then red in the autumn, and there are terminal trusses of purplish-red, pink, lilac or white flowers, 3-4 cm long, with six wavy petals; "Little Chief" is a dwarf variety.
*L. speciosa*, Pride of India, from China and India, has leaves 10-20 cm long, striking flowers 5-7 cm across, which are pale pink

at first and later turn dark purple, and 100-200 stamens.
This shrub is suitable only for a very sunny spot sheltered from the rain, for example, against a whitewashed, south-facing wall.
It requires a mixture of three parts potting compost to one part clay or loam, with some organic manure. During the growing season, water liberally several times a week, and apply liquid manure once a fortnight. Prune back regularly, and before overwintering in a cool, and frost-free place, 2-5° C. Prune back hard to ensure the plant flowers profusely and retains its shape. The plant flowers on young wood. Place in the light after repotting in March/April: young plants every two years, older plants every 5-10 years, damaging the clump as little as possible. Propagate from cuttings in April/May. They form roots in a warm place. The Japanese dwarf variety can be propagated from seed at approximately 20° C. Sensitive to mildew.

*Lantana camara*

# Lantana

⚘ ↕ 30-150 ↔ 60 cm ⊘ ⊛ ⬚

*Lantana*, is indigenous in (sub)tropical South Africa, America and the West Indies, and comprises more than 150 species. The plants were already being cultivated in Leiden and in botanical gardens in England in about 1700.
This is a woody shrub, often covered in coarse hair, and with a thorny trunk. It has whorls of serrated, often wrinkled leaves, which emit a strong fragrance when touched. The fairly small flowers grow in compact clusters on stems in the leaf axilla or terminally; they have a small calyx, and funnel-shaped corolla ending in four or five spreading lobes.
*L. camara* is a sturdy shrub with oval-oblong, wrinkled leaves, 2.5-12 cm long, hairy like the stems, and flat, yellow or orange clusters of flowers, 2.5-6 cm across, which turn red.
*Lantana* hybrids have more or less the same characteristics as the species, but are more compact and have more clusters of flowers in all sorts of colours, including white. They are more resistant to rain.
*L. montevidensis* has thin, hanging stems, and pinky-lilac flowers in long-stemmed clusters, 3 cm across.
This plant is suitable for a light, sunny spot, out of bright sunlight. It is also suitable as a small tree. Water regularly, adding plant food to the water every ten days.
Overwinter in a light, frost-free place at approximately 5° C. Water less, and do not feed. Repot in spring in ordinary potting compost and prune back.
Propagate from seed in early spring; take cuttings and place young, pruned top cuttings in moist peat to take root at 20-25° C.

# Laurus
## *Laurel*

🌱 ↕ 1-6 m ○ ⊘ ◉ ✤ ✿ 5 ✂

*Laurus* is indigenous in eastern Mediterranean regions *(L. nobilis)*, and on the Canary Islands, the Azores and Madeira *(L. azorica)*. It comprises only two species. This is a woody evergreen shrub or tree with aromatic leaves, which are used both for medicinal purposes (liquorice) and in the kitchen. In the past it was used for making laurel wreaths. The wood is hard and tough. In this part of the world only *L. nobilis* is cultivated; under the right conditions it can grow hundreds of years old.

*L. nobilis*, laurel, is a branching shrub with leathery, oblong-oval leaves, 6-12 cm long. The small, pale yellow flowers are usually dioecious and grow close together in the leaf axilla; female specimens produce green berries the size of a cherry, which later turn almost black. *L. nobilis* "Angustifolia" has narrow leaves with wavy edges; "Aurea" has yellowish-green leaves.

This plant can grow in the sun or in a more or less shady spot. Water liberally during the growing period, adding liquid feed once a week. It can tolerate a few degrees of frost. Overwinter at a minimum of 2° C, not necessarily in a light place, but well ventilated. Water less, but do not allow to dry out. Prune back in spring and autumn to retain shape. It tolerates pruning very well and can therefore be pruned in many shapes which can take years to achieve. For culinary use, cut mature leaves in autumn and dry in the shade. Repot in spring every five years in potting compost with extra loam and some well-rotted cow manure. Propagate from top cuttings in September, or from seed. Very sensitive to scale insects. Spray regularly with water as a preventative measure.

# Lavatera
## *Tree mallow*

○ ↕ 60-150 ↔ 30-80 ○ ⊘ ✿ 6-9

*Lavatera* is indigenous from the Mediterranean Sea to the Himalayas, on the Canary Islands, in California and Australia. These are annual and biennial herbaceous plants, or perennial (sub-)shrubs, often hairy, with large, striking, usually white, red, pink, or lavender-coloured flowers, or sometimes yellow flowers. It has a five-lobed calyx, like the spreading corolla which closes when it wilts. The stamens are fused together, except at the top, and at the bottom of every bloom there is a leafy,

*Laurus nobilis, Laurel*

fused extra calyx which distinguishes the species from the *Malva* species, which have an extra calyx consisting of one to three separate leaflets. The kidney-shaped achenes appear after flowering.

*L. thuringiaca* from southern Europe is a perennial herbaceous plant with serrated, oval-lanceolate leaves, the top one of which is three-lobed, and pale, pinkish-red flowers 5-6 cm across; *L. thuringiaca* "Barnsley" is a selection with large flowers. Good for cut flowers.

*L. assurgentiflora* is an evergreen shrub from California with five to seven-lobed leaves up to 15 cm long, and long-stemmed, pale, purplish-red flowers with darker veins, 5-7 cm across.

*L. trimestris* is a sturdy, erect plant with large, satiny flowers in short terminal clusters; "Mont Blanc", white; "Sunset" (syn. "Loveliness"), dark pink flowers. Good for cut flowers.

This plant needs a sunny spot with nutritious soil. Water liberally and add liquid feed once every two weeks when the buds appear. Propagate from cuttings and seed.

*Lavatera thuringiaca, Tree mallow*

# Leonotis

• ○ ↕ 50-180 ↔ -150 ○ ❀ 8-9 ▽

*Leonotis* is indigenous particularly in South Africa, but also in other tropical areas. It comprises 30-40 species. *L. leonurus* was grown in this part of the world as early as 1663. These are annual herbaceous plants and perennial shrubs with squarish stems, whorls of oval-lanceolate leaves, and whorls of white to orange flowers, curving upwards in the top leaf axilla. They have a two-lipped corolla with a hairy upper lip spreading outwards.

*L. leonurus*, lion's ear, is a fairly tall shrub with grey hairy stems, short-stemmed, coarsely serrated, lanceolate leaves, 5-10 cm long, and an orange, woolly, hairy flowerhead, 4-6 cm long, more than three times as long as the serrated calyx; the lower lip soon wilts; "Albiflora", white flowers.

*L. nepetifolia* is less tall, with broad oval leaves up to 10 cm long on long stems and yellow to orangey-red flowers, 2.5 cm long, with thorny supporting leaves in compact, spherical whorls up to 10 cm across.

This plant is suitable for a sunny spot protected against bright sunlight. It requires well-drained, nutritious soil and usually some support. Water regularly, adding liquid feed to the water once a week during the growing period. Prune after flowering. Overwinter in a frost-free place, not below 5° C. Pinch out tips of young plants two or three times for bushy growth. Propagate from seed and cuttings in winter or early spring.

*Leonotis leonurus*

*Leptospermum scoparium*

*Leptospermum lanigerum*

# Leptospermum

🌿 ↕ 1-3 m ↔ 1-3 m ○ ⚙ 4-7 🏺

*Leptospermum* is indigenous in Australia, New Zealand and Tasmania, and comprises about 50 species. The wood of *L. scoparium* is used for the handles of tools; the leaves were used for tea by the first Australian colonists ("tea tree").
These are evergreen shrubs with small, smooth-edged, leathery leaves on thin stems, and white, pink or red flowers.
*L. lanigerum* (syn. *L. pubescens*) is a broad, branching shrub. The young stems and leaves are covered with woolly hair; the leaves are usually greyish-green and up to 2 cm long; it has white flowers.
*L. scoparium*, Manuka, is a variable species with aromatic leaves, which flowers profusely, originally with white flowers. It has pointed leaves up to 1 cm long, and there are many cultivars with pink, lilac-pink or red flowers, also with double or semi-double flowers, e.g., "Kiwi", crimson; "Nicholisii", dark red flowers, bronze-purplish leaves; "Red Damast", double bright red flowers.
This plant is suitable for a sheltered, sunny spot. During the growing season water liberally with soft water. Feed now and again (half concentration). After flowering, regularly cut back young stems to two-thirds of the length. Overwinter in a light, cool spot at 5-12° C, certainly no warmer. If the plant dries out, it loses its leaves. Repot in deep pots with well-drained, lime-free soil, e.g., a mixture of leaf-mould, potting compost and garden peat, or so-called Azalea soil. Propagate from top cuttings in August, which take root under glass in a mixture of sieved peat with some sharp sand. It can also be propagated from seed.

# Limonium
*Sea lavender*

○ ↕ 80-125 m ↔ -60 ○ ⚙ 8-9 🏺

*Limonium* is indigenous in a very large area, and comprises about 300 species, of which *L. vulgare*, sea lavender, is found on the coast in this part of the world. The plants have salt glands to secrete excessive salt in periods of drought. Some shrub-like species are suitable for cultivation in tubs.
These annual or perennial, herbaceous or

woody-stemmed plants usually form rosettes of single, smooth-edged, slightly leathery leaves. They have flowerheads consisting of five flowers surrounded by bracts. They are suitable for cut flowers, especially dried flowers, because they keep their colour well.
*L. brassicifolium* (syn. *Statice brassicifolia*), from the Canary Islands, is a shrub-like plant with leaves 25-30 cm long, flowering stems with spreading wings, and compound clusters of flowers with a bluish-purple calyx and yellowish-white corolla.
*L. macrophyllum* (syn. *Statice macrophyllum*) is a shrub-like plant with flowering stems with broad wings, oval-spatulate, slightly hairy leaves up to 30 cm long, and flowers with a purple calyx and yellowish-white corolla.
This plant is suitable for a sunny spot in large pots with well-drained soil.
Overwinter at 5° C with little water, but do not allow to dry out.
Propagate from seed, by dividing plant, and from cuttings.

*Limonium, Sea lavender*

# Lobelia

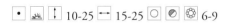
• ⚘ ↕ 10-25 ↔ 15-25 ○ ⊘ ✿ 6-9

*Lobelia* is indigenous particularly in tropical and subtropical regions and comprises 200-300 species, of which *L. dortmanna*, water lobelia, is sometimes found in shallow peat bogs in this part of the world.
This is an annual or perennial, herbaceous plant with spreading leaves, and blue, red or white flowers, with two narrow and three broad petals which grow singly or in terminal flowerheads.
*L. erinus*, cultivated as an annual, is a low-growing plant with narrow, lanceolate leaves, and flowers approximately 2 cm across in terminal clusters. There are many cultivars, e.g., "Cambridge Blue", azure blue; "Rosamund", burgundy with a white centre; "Blue Cascade", light blue, pendent flowers; very suitable for ground cover in larger tubs or hanging baskets.
*L. laxiflora* is an evergreen, shrub-like plant with narrow, serrated, lanceolate leaves, and tubular red and yellow flowers, 4 cm long, in the axilla of the upper leaves, growing on a long, thin, flowering stem. Overwinter in a frost-free spot.
This plant requires fairly moist soil, rich in humus. Water liberally in warm weather.
Propagate from seed in March in heated conditions.

*Lobelia erinus "Cambridge Blue"*

*Lupinus arboreus, Lupin*

# Lupinus
*Lupin*

○ ⚘ ↕ 1-2 m ↔ 1-2 m ○ ✳ 6-8

*Lupinus* is indigenous in Mediterranean regions and North America, and comprises approximately 200 species. The Ancient Greeks ate the cooked seeds of *L. albus* as long ago as 400 BC.
These are annual or perennial plants which grow particularly in sandy, rather acid soil. They have attractive, deeply indented, palmate leaves, and short-stemmed, characteristic pea-like flowers consisting of five petals, in rosettes or long, spreading clusters. These are followed with long pods with round or flat seeds.
*L. arboreus*, the tree lupin, is a fast-growing, branching sub-shrub from California. The undersides of the leaves are covered with silvery-white hair, and the sulphur-yellow loose spikes of flowers are 15-25 cm long and smell of honey. There are several cultivars; they are resistant to sea wind.

*Lupinus* hybrids, perennial plants, are lower and flower profusely with single or bicoloured flowers, e.g., "Chandelier", golden-yellow flowers; "My Castle", red; "Noblemaiden", white; "The Chatelaine", white and pink; "The Governor", white and blue.
This plant is suitable for a sunny, sheltered spot with dry, lime-free soil. It is resistant to drought, but does better in more nutritious soil with more water. Remove dead flowers and overwinter in a frost-free place. It does not live long, but is easy to propagate from seed. Seeds should be pre-soaked in tepid water. Flowers in the second season. It can also be propagated from summer cuttings.

# Malvaviscus

◦ ↕ 1.5-3 m ○ ✿ winter ▨ ✄

*Malvaviscus* is indigenous in the warmer parts of America, and comprises about 20 species, of which *M. arborescens* is the main one to be cultivated.

This deep-rooted shrub has spreading leaves. It has a long flowering period, and produces bright red, often pendent flowers with five partially overlapping petals, stamens fused in a tube, protruding beyond the corolla, and an even longer pistil.

*M. arborescens* has leaves 5-10 cm long and wide, with a serrated leaf margin, and erect flowers, 2.5 cm long. The natural variety, *mexicanus* (syn. *M. penduliflorus*, *M. grandiflorus*), has pendent flowers, 3-5 cm long; there is also a cultivar with pale pink flowers.

This plant is suitable for a light, sunny spot and can also be cultivated as a small tree. It requires some extra loam in the potting compost. Keep the clump moderately moist and feed with liquid plant food every ten days. Prune back hard after flowering, and overwinter at 10-15° C, or slightly warmer, but then it should be regularly sprayed (to prevent scale insects and whitefly).

Minimum temperature, 5° C, or the leaves will drop off. Propagate from cuttings, which take root at 20-23° C, or from seed.

*Malvaviscus arborescens var. mexicanus "Albus"*

*Malvaviscus arborescens var. mexicanus*

Matthiola incana
"Brompton", Stock

# Matthiola
*Stock*

•• ○ ↕ 30-75 ↔ 20-45 ○ ◉ ❀3-6

*Matthiola* is particularly indigenous in
Mediterranean regions and comprises 55
species. This is an annual, biennial or
perennial, herbaceous plant, usually covered
with grey hair, and with spikes of pink,
purple, yellow or white flowers. They are
cultivated for their fragrant double flowers.
The stamens and pistil develop into petals,
and consequently these plants do not
produce fruits.

*M. incana*, Brompton stock, is an annual or
perennial, stiff, upright plant, covered with
silvery-grey hair. It has spatulate leaves,
fragrant, pink, purplish-pink or white,
fragrant flowers, followed by long, narrow
siliqua. There are many varieties with
flowers in different shapes and colours,
lengths of spike and flowering times.
There are also shrub-like varieties and dwarf
varieties, often suitable for cut flowers. For
the garden there are summer stocks, and for
growing in the greenhouse there are winter
stocks which flower in spring. *M. incana*
hybrids are suitable for sowing in pots, then
standing outside in summer in a sunny spot,
in lime-rich, nutritious, moist soil. It is
sensitive to moisture (root rot). Propagate
from seed in February/March, in heated
conditions under glass.

Matthiola incana
Cindarella Apple
Blossom, Stock

# Mirabilis
*Four 'o clock flower*

○ ↕ 30-130 ↔ 50-100 ○ ✿ 6-10

*Mirabilis* is indigenous in Central and South America, and comprises 60 species. Mirabilis means "miraculous", and this is based on the fact that a single plant can produce flowers of different colours, although this rarely happens. The fragrant flowers open in the afternoon and only close towards the beginning of the following day, which explains its common name.
These are annual or perennial, herbaceous plants, with a thick, tuberous root, bushy growth with slightly hairy, fleshy stems, and whorls of oval, pointed leaves. It has red, pink, white and yellow or striped flowers which grow in groups of three to six.

The corolla consists of a tube, 2-3 cm long, with a wide, spreading margin. After flowering, the plant forms fairly large black seeds. The parts above the ground die off every year.
*M. jalapa*, Marvel of Peru, is the most commonly cultivated species from Mexico. It flowers profusely; "Tea Time Yellow" has yellow flowers.
*M. longiflora* is up to 90 cm tall, with greyish-green, lanceolate leaves and sticky, white, pink or purple flowers with a tubular corolla, 12 cm long, which are fragrant at night.
This plant is suitable for a sunny spot in nutritious soil, preferably with some clay. The tubers should be overwintered in a frost-free place, like dahlias.
Propagate from seed, by dividing the plant, or from root cuttings.

*Mirabilis jalapa "Mixed"*

51

*Myrtus communis*

# Myrtus
*Myrtle*

⚟ ↕ 1.2-3 m ↔ 90-150 ○ ⊘ ✿ 7-9 ⊕

*Myrtus* is indigenous particularly in
(sub)tropical regions of Australia and
America, and comprises approximately 100
species. The oil from the leaves was used in
the past as a perfume. These evergreen
shrubs have whorls of leathery leaves and
white, usually single flowers.
*M. communis*, common myrtle, is one of the
oldest known plants to be grown in tubs.
It is a tall, bushy shrub with reddish-brown
stems, shiny green, lanceolate,
short-stemmed, very aromatic leaves,
2.5-5 cm long, and single, white, fragrant
flowers, approximately 2 cm across, with
5 petals and numerous long, white stamens.
The small, purplish-black edible berries
appear after the plant has flowered.
*M. communis* var. *tarentina* ("Jenny
Reitenbach") has narrow leaves and white
fruits; it tolerates slight frost; "Variegata"
has greyish-green leaves with a white margin.

This plant is suitable for a sunny, sheltered
spot, even in coastal areas. Water regularly
with soft water. It is easy to prune and is
suitable for growing as a small tree or for
topiary work. Regularly pinch out the tips
of young plants. Overwinter in a frost-free,
light, well-ventilated place at 5-12° C. It is
sensitive to artificial fertilizers, and should
be repotted every year in acid soil, rich in
humus, e.g., potting compost with some
peat and clay. Propagate from top cuttings
of non-flowering shoots (January or July),
which take root under glass in heated
conditions, in peat with some sand.

*Nandina domestica*

# Nandina

⚘ ↕ 1-2.5 m ↔ 1 m ⊘ ✿ 7 ❀

*Nandina*, comes from Japan and China and comprises only one species, *N. domestica*, the Latin form of the Japanese name, nanten. *N. domestica*, heavenly bamboo, is an evergreen shrub with a large number of upright, unbranching, bamboo-like stems, bipinnate or tripinnate leaves, 30-50 cm long, consisting of narrow, smooth-edged leaflets, 2-8 cm long, tapering to a point, and insignificant white flowers, 0.5 cm across, in terminal panicles up to 30 cm long. The ornamental value lies particularly in the abundance of bright red berries, which appear after a warm summer and remain on the shrub for a long time; "Alba" has white berries; "Nana purpurea" has purplish, young leaves.
This plant is suitable for a light spot with well-drained moist soil, mixed with a lot of organic material. Water regularly to keep the clump moist, and apply liquid feed once a fortnight during the growing period. Overwinter frost-free at 7-10° C, with little water. Propagate from seed or top cuttings in August, in a moist atmosphere, using rooting powder (not easy).

53

*Nerium oleander hybrid*

*Nerium oleander*

# Nerium
*Oleander*

⚘ ↕ 1-6 m ↔ -3 m ○ ✤ 5-9 !

*Nerium* was originally indigenous from southern Europe, across Asia to southwest China. It is currently thought to comprise three species, one of which is cultivated. The stems and leaves contain a poisonous, milky juice which can irritate the skin. *N. oleander*, oleander, has been cultivated for centuries. It is a woody-stemmed, evergreen plant with whorls or rosettes of three leathery, smooth-edged, lanceolate, green or greyish-green leaves, 10-15 cm long, with a pronounced main vein, and terminal, branching clusters of white, pink, salmon, light or dark yellow flowers with five petals fused in a tubular corolla at the base, and five stamens. There are also varieties with scented or unscented, semi-double and double flowers. It is resistant to sea air, air pollution and some night frost.

Suitable for a very sunny spot; protect against too much rain. If possible, grow in plastic pots to prevent drying out; it requires a great deal of water, depending on the weather. During the growing season apply liquid feed (half concentration) every other week. Prune in spring to promote flowering. Overwinter in a cool, light, airy spot at 5-10° C. Water sparingly. Yellow and dark red varieties, particularly with double flowers, require higher temperatures, 10-16° C. When the temperature rises, give more water. Repot young plants annually in potting compost with some old cow manure. For older plants, replace the top layer. Propagate in June by placing semi-woody cuttings with two or three pairs of leaves in water; plant in pots when they have taken root. Sow at 20-25° C, as soon as the seed is ripe (limited germination). Pinch out tips of young plants regularly. Sensitive to scale insects and red spider mite.

# Olearia
*Daisy bush*

⚘ ↕ 2-4.5 m ○ ✤ 6-8

*Olearia* is indigenous in the southern hemisphere, particularly in Australia and New Zealand, and comprises 100 species.

These are woody-stemmed, evergreen shrubs which flower profusely and will tolerate some degrees of frost. They usually have spreading, leathery, shiny green leaves with a white or brown, hairy underside, and flowers in umbel-like clusters. The flowerheads consist of tubular flowers surrounded by a ring of long ray flowers.
*O. avicennifolia* is a shrub with felty stems, greyish-green leaves, 5-12 cm long, and small, white flowers. It flowers in late summer.
*O. x haastii*, is a cross of *O. avicennifolia* and *O. moschata*, a bushy shrub with small, dark green leaves up to 2.5 cm long, and flat clusters of small, white, fragrant flowers with a yellow heart, which flower from July to August.
*O. macrodonta* has shiny, greyish-green, holly-like, wavy and sharply-toothed leaves up to 12 cm long, and white flowers with a reddish tinge, up to 1 cm across, which appear in June.
This shrub is suitable for a sunny, sheltered spot. It tolerates (sea) winds, and requires nutritious, well-drained soil, rich in lime and humus. Overwinter in a light, airy, cool place. Propagate from cuttings of herbaceous side shoots in late summer, which form roots in heated conditions.

*Olearia macrodonta, Daisy bush*

*Oxypetalum coeruleum*

# Oxypetalum

○ ↕ 100 ○ ✿ 6-7 !

*Oxypetalum* (syn. *Tweedia*) is indigenous in South America from Mexico to Brazil, and comprises 150 species of perennial, herbaceous plants or sub-shrubs, although only one of these is cultivated.
*O. caeruleum* (syn. *Tweedia caeruleum*) is a herbaceous plant, slightly woody-stemmed at the bottom, with limp stems and short-stemmed, oval leaves with a heart-shaped base. The short-stemmed clusters of flowers in the leaf axilla have pink buds, but are sky-blue when they open, and then turn dark blue. They have a short, tubular corolla ending in five lobes, and a fleshy, dark, extra corolla. The plant contains a poisonous milky juice.
It requires a sunny, warm spot, some support, and well-drained potting compost which is kept moist at all times. Feed once a month. Overwinter at a minimum of 12-15° C with high humidity. Repot in spring, pinch out tips several times and prune back older specimens (wear gloves). Propagate from seed in March and harden off slowly.

*Pelargonium peltatum*
*"Summer Showers"*

*Pelargonium x hortorum*
*"Vogue series"*

# Pelargonium

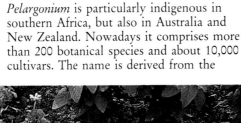
4-10

*Pelargonium* is particularly indigenous in southern Africa, but also in Australia and New Zealand. Nowadays it comprises more than 200 botanical species and about 10,000 cultivars. The name is derived from the

Greek word "palargos" (= stork) because the fruit looks like a long, pointed (stork's) beak.
*Pelargonium* is often confused with *Geranium*, another genus in the same family, and it was originally classified under this genus.
This is an annual or perennial, herbaceous or evergreen, slightly woody-stemmed plant which usually flowers profusely and sometimes has underground tubers which can grow to a great size, as in *P. triste*.
It has spreading leaves, usually indented, sometimes with smooth edges, and flowers with five petals and ten stamens, seven of which have an anther. The ripe fruits split into five parts with one seed.
*P. x domesticum* (formerly *grandiflorum* hybrids), French geranium, are house plants which are only suitable outdoors if not hung in the rain.
*P. x hortorum* (formerly *zonal* hybrids), garden geraniums, are particularly crosses of *P. inquinans* and *P. zonale*; there are many cultivars with single, double or semi-double flowers which flower for a long time, in all sorts of combinations of white, pink, red, salmon, orange and purple. There are also varieties with coloured leaves.
*P. peltatum*, hanging geraniums and ivies are creeping plants with stems up to 100 cm long, thick leaves and fairly small umbels of single or double flowers, 2.5 cm across; there are also varieties with coloured leaves. Fragrant species and cultivars usually have small flowers, e.g., *P. crispum*, which has twisted, lemon-scented leaves; *P. x fragrans* has a smell of nutmeg; *P. tomentosum* smells of peppermint.

*top:*
*Pelargonium x domesticum hybrida*

These plants require a fairly cool spot in the sun or semi-shade. Water moderately, always waiting until the clump goes dry. When it is very warm, mist occasionally in the evening. Prune down to the third eye in spring for compact growth. Deadhead flowers halfway down the flowering stem. Turn plants regularly to maintain their shape and to prevent roots from becoming potbound. Overwinter virtually dry at a minimum of 7° C. Repot once a year in spring at the same time as pruning the plant, into well-drained potting compost with some clay in fairly small pots, so that the roots spread out. Do not feed. Propagate from seed or cuttings, using top cuttings, 6-7 cm long. After removing the lower leaves, place in a mixture of one part potting compost to two parts sharp sand.

# Petunia

• ⬍ 20-30 ↔ 30 (or more) ○ ✿ 6-9

*Petunia* is indigenous in the warmer regions of North and South America, and comprises about 30-40 species.
This is an annual or perennial, herbaceous plant, completely covered with soft, sticky hairs, with smooth-edged, oval leaves, and single, trumpet-shaped, red, violet or white flowers in the leaf axilla, with a calyx divided into five parts, and five unequal stamens.
*P. x hybrida* cultivars come in every shade of red, violet, blue, pink, salmon, yellow and white, and there are even bicoloured varieties. They can be divided into smooth-edged selections with small, large, single, double or pendent flowers, and fringed selections with single or double flowers. There are always many constantly changing selections available: "Grandiflora", enormous selections with very large, single or double flowers, often fringed; "Multiflora", many medium, single or double flowers resistant to the weather; "Pendula", pendent flowers.
This plant is suitable for a slightly sheltered spot in full sunlight. It requires nutritious soil. Water liberally, though it is fairly resistant to drought. Too much plant food results in many leaves and few flowers. Deadhead plants regularly. Propagate from seed: early at 18-20° C for early flowering, and from cuttings (varieties with double flowers).

*Petunia x hybrida "Rose and White Pearls"*

*Petunia x hybrida "Purple Pirouette"*

top: *Phormium tenax, New Zealand flax*

# Phormium
*New Zealand flax*

○ ↕ 0.3-2 m ↔ 1-1.5 m ○ ◉ ✦ 7-8 (rarely)

*Phormium* is indigenous in New Zealand, and comprises two species with hybrids and many cultivars. It was first cultivated in Europe towards the end of the 18th century. The leaves of *P. tenax* contain tough fibres which were used by the Maoris for braiding, clothes, mats, rope, etc.
This is a perennial, herbaceous, evergreen plant with long, sword-shaped, red, purple or bronze leaves which grow directly from the thick rhizome. It is resistant to fluctuations in temperature, air pollution, and even a few degrees of frost.
The beautiful leaves are suitable for cutting.
*P. tenax*, New Zealand flax, is a sturdy species which grows wild in slightly moist soil. It has stiff leaves up to 2 m long and 8-10 cm wide, with a sharp point. *P. tenax* "Atropurpureum" has purple leaves; "Aureum" has broad, yellow stripes.
*P. colensoi* (syn. *P. cookianum*) is a compact plant up to 1 m tall, with undulating, dark green leaves up to 6 cm wide. *P. colensoi* "Tricolor" has coloured leaves, creamy-yellow with red stripes and margins. Hybrids include *Phormium* "Apricot Queen", which has curving, creamy-yellow leaves with a dark green margin, 90 cm long; "Dazzler", approximately 75 cm tall, slow-growing, with narrow, overhanging, red and purple striped leaves; "Duet", a dwarf variety with green and cream leaves, 30 cm long.
This plant is suitable for a sunny spot in nutritious soil, consisting of two parts potting compost, one part clay, and some old cow manure; large varieties need quite a lot of water, small varieties need less. During the growing period apply liquid plant food every fourteen days. Overwinter at 5-10° C in a light spot. Propagate by dividing the plant in early March.
It can also be propagated from seed, but it quickly loses its power to germinate.

*left:*
*Phormium tenax "Purpureum"*

# Phygelius

⊡ ⊡ 90-150 ↔ 50 ◯ ✿ 7-10

*Phygelius* is indigenous in South Africa and comprises two species. This is a small, deciduous sub-shrub, with winged stems and whorls of serrated leaves on stems. The flowers have a calyx divided into five parts, and a long, tube-shaped corolla with protruding stamens and pistil.

*P. aequalis* is a compact shrub with salmon-coloured flowers with petals which do not curve outwards; *P. aequalis* "Yellow Trumpet" has cream-coloured or pale yellow, tubular flowers, and often flowers a second time.

*P. capensis* has coral red flowers, hanging down as buds, and gradually curving upwards into a horizontal position, forming an open, clustered flowerhead. They are suitable as cut flowers; *P. capensis* "Coccineus" has triangular leaves and large, scarlet flowers which easily drop off.

This is an excellent plant for a sunny, sheltered spot in tubs, though it is better dug into the open soil; it is resistant to drought, and with a thick cover it can be left in the soil for the winter in a sheltered spot, though it is better to overwinter it frost-free in a light place. Repot in spring in nutritious, well-drained soil. Propagate from top cuttings in early summer, which form roots at 20° C. It can also be propagated from seed.

*Phygelius aequalis "Yellow Trumpet"*

*Phygelius capensis*

*Plumbago auriculata,*
*Leadwort*

# Plumbago
## *Leadwort*

⌖ ↕ 1-2.5 m ↔ 0.8-1.5 m ⊘ ✿ 5-10

*Plumbago auriculata*
*"Alba"*

*Plumbago* is indigenous in tropical and subtropical regions, and comprises about 12 species, some of which are cultivated as ornamental plants. The juice of some species can be used to treat blisters.

This is a herbaceous or woody-stemmed, semi-deciduous plant with long, twining stems which tend to climb, spreading leaves, and blue, red or white flowers in five parts.

*P. auriculata* (syn. *P. capensis*), Cape leadwort, from South Africa, is an upright shrub with limp stems which tend to climb, short-stemmed, narrow, oval leaves, 5 cm long, and clusters of up to 20 sky-blue flowers about 3 cm across in umbels. Every petal has a darker stripe, and the sticky, hairy calyx tends to stick to clothes.

The plant flowers on the young shoots, even at an early age; *P. auriculata* "Alba" has white flowers.

This plant requires a light, sunny spot and some support. It needs nutritious, well-drained soil. Water liberally and apply liquid plant food once a fortnight. Cut stems which have finished flowering to encourage more flowering. Prune before the start of the winter rest, pruning back long, limp stems considerably. Do not allow the clump to dry out in winter. 5-8° C is fine, but warmer temperatures up to 14° C are also possible. Repot young plants every year; later, every 3-5 years, in large, well-drained pots in a mixture of potting compost, one part clay and some old cow manure. Propagate from semi-woody, summer cuttings which take root at 20-25° C.

# Punica granatum
*Pomegranate*

🌿 ↕ 1-3 m ↔ 1-2 m ○ ✿ 6-9

*Punica* probably originated from India and became widespread in Mediterranean regions. It comprises two species, of which only *P. granatum* is cultivated. The Romans knew it as the "Punic apple"; it was believed to have a purifying action which could be because of its slight purgative effect. The fruit is used to make grenadine; the bark contains lye.

*P. granatum*, the pomegranate, often has thorny branches, lanceolate, leathery, shiny green leaves, and scarlet, trumpet-shaped flowers up to 4 cm long, which grow terminally or in groups of two or three on the young stems, and have a tubular calyx, and an often slightly frizzy corolla protruding beyond the calyx. Much older plants flower more profusely. A sunny summer and fairly dry autumn increase the chance of fruits which are 6-12 cm in diameter, with a tough, leathery, yellowish-red peel and consist of a large number of segments with one seed surrounded by a red layer which is edible and has a sharp, sweet or sour taste. The "crown" of the fruit is the leathery calyx, which remains behind. Cultivars with double flowers and different colours do not usually bear fruit. *P. granatum* "Nana" is a dwarf variety up to 1 m tall and broad, which bears many small fruits even at a very young age.

This plant is suitable for a sheltered spot. After gradually becoming habituated to more sun (burning), it can be moved into full sunlight. Water regularly and feed from time to time. It tolerates temperatures down to -10° C, but not excessive moisture, so it is best to place it inside in winter in a cool place (approximately 5° C). Prune back before this, pruning young twigs to half their length. In older specimens also remove some larger branches to promote the growth of young wood. Do not allow the clump to dry out. Repot carefully (do not damage roots) in spring: young plants every year, older plants every five years, in ordinary potting compost with one-third part clay. Propagate from seed, or from cuttings in February/March using woody cuttings of stems with a heel 10 cm long, or later in the year from leafy top cuttings which take root in a mixture of peat and sand at 25-30° C.

*Punica granatum "Legrellei"*

*Punica granatum "Nana"*

top: *Rosa "Händel"*
bottom: *Rosa "New Dawn"*

# Rosa
*Rose*

*Rosa* is indigenous in temperate regions of the northern hemisphere. It is a very common genus, comprising about 250 species, of which 45 are found in Europe. In China, roses were already cultivated in 2700 BC. These are deciduous shrubs, usually thorny, and usually with compound leaves. The flowers have 4-5 sepals and petals, many stamens and pistils, and grow singly or in clusters. The single-seed fruits are collected together in the rosehip, an extended receptacle which contains a lot of vitamin C. It is used for jam making and is very popular with birds. Rose oil is extracted from the petals, particularly of *R. damascena*. Many cultivars of *Rosa* are suitable for growing in tubs, such as polyantha roses, which have large clusters of small, early-flowering blooms and long-flowering, miniature roses, 25-50 cm tall, of which there are about 200 varieties. In general, roses require a sunny spot, potting compost with compost and old cow manure, and quite a lot of water. Plant so that the bud union is approximately 5 cm below ground level. Always prune back above an eye which faces outwards, so that new growth is also outwards, even in standard roses. Remove wildshoots at the base, or the rose will grow out of control. Deadhead regularly to promote flowering. Propagation is fairly difficult, as budding and grafting are the most suitable ways of propagating these cultivars.

⟂ 1.2-2.4 m ↔ 0.9-1.5 m ◯ ◉ ✺ 5-8

*Botanical roses*
Several flowers in small sprays, often with striking red or black rosehips; can be propagated from seed (autumn), wildshoots or summer cuttings.
*R. hugonensis*, bright yellow, extremely early flowering; *R. movesii*, blood-red, June, with orangey-red rosehips; *R. pimpinellifolia* (syn. *R. spinosissima*), Burnet rose, a low-growing rose with creamy-white flowers and small, black rosehips.

⟂ 75-150 cm ↔ 45-75 cm ◯ ◉ ✺ 6-8

*Floribunda and tea roses*
These usually have semi-double or double flowers in sprays. Prune back more than

other varieties, and remove old sprays of
flowers in autumn. In spring, prune back all
branches to 15 cm from the ground.
Floribunda "All Gold", dark golden-yellow;
"Dearest", salmon-pink; "Iceberg", pure
white; "Topsi", a dwarf variety up to 45 cm
tall, bright orangey-red. Tea roses have
large, very fragrant flowers: "Blue Moon",
first pink, later lilac; "King's Ransom",
bright yellow; "Ernest H. Morse", bright
red; "Melrose", cream with a red blush.

⊥ -3 m ↔ 0.9-1.5 m ◯ ◉ ❀ 6-8

*Climbing and weeping roses*, double or single
flowers, growing singly or in small sprays.
Climbing roses: prune back main branches
to 50 cm, side branches to 10 cm; tie back
main branches. "Danse de Feu", double,
bright red flowers; "Golden Showers",
double, golden-yellow flowers; "Händel",
semi-double, white flowers with a red
margin; "New Dawn", strong, semi-double,
light pink flowers.
*Weeping roses:*
Prune back to 30 cm above the ground;
after flowering, remove some of the stems
which have finished flowering to create
room for young shoots, which are tied back,
sometimes to the main stem. "Albéric
Barbier" is a vigorous plant with
semi-double, creamy-yellow, apple-scented
flowers; "Dorothy Perkins" has double,
bright pink flowers; "Sanders White",
double, pure white flowers.

*top: Rosa pimpinellifolia "Frühlingszauber"*

*Bush roses*
Old fashioned:

 1.2-1.8 m ↔ 0.9-1.2 m ◯ ◉ ❀ 6-7

Fragrant, semi-double or double flowers,
slightly flattened. Also moss roses (the name
refers to the green growths on the buds);
"Cardinal de Richelieu", red, folded petals;
"Königin von Dänemark", crimson; "Nuits
de Young", small, dark red flowers.

Modern:

⊥ 1.2-2.1 m ↔ 0.9-1.5 m ◯ ◉ ❀ 6-8

From low, compact to tall, airy varieties;
single (semi-)double, sometimes decorative
rosehips; "Marigold", dark yellow,
semi-double, fragrant.

*right:*
*Rosa "Golden Showers"*

*Rosmarinus officinalis,*
*Rosemary*

# Rosmarinus
*Rosemary*

⚘ ↕ 90-150 ○ ✿ 5-6 ⬚

*Rosmarinus* comprises three species, of which *R. officinalis*, rosemary, has been cultivated as a medicinal and culinary herb since ancient times.
This is an evergreen, small, bushy shrub which is not really winter-hardy in this part of the world. It has felted, hairy stems, narrow, oblong leaves curled in at the edges, shiny green on the upper side and felted-grey on the underside, and pale blue or almost white, two-lipped flowers which grow in groups in the leaf axilla on one-year-old wood.
*R. officinalis* "Albus", white flowers; "Marjocan Pink", pink; "Benenden Blue", blue and low-growing; "Sissinghurst Blue", dark blue.
This plant is suitable for a sunny, warm, sheltered spot, not too much rain.
It tolerates drought fairly well, and can be grown outside on the coast. It tolerates frost down to -10° C. Otherwise overwinter in a cool, very light place. Repot every three years in well-drained, lime-rich soil, e.g., potting compost with clay. No extra manure is needed. Prune back regularly after flowering or in spring.
Propagate from seed, or from cuttings with a heel in August/September, which take root in a cold frame.

# Solanum
## Nightshade

🌿 ↕ 40-90 ○ ◉ ✿ 6-8 ! ❀

Solanum is found all over the world and comprises about 1700 species, of which many are well-known food crops, such as the potato and aubergine.

This is an annual, biennial or perennial, herbaceous or woody-stemmed plant with striking flowers consisting of a star-shaped crown in five parts, with yellow, fused stamens surrounding the style in the centre. All the fruits, including the aubergine, are berries; the unripe fruits are often poisonous.

S. glaucum, from South America, has smooth, narrow, oblong, pointed, smooth-edged leaves, 10-15 cm long, blue, star-shaped flowers, 2.5 cm across, in terminal clusters, and purple fruits, 2 cm long.

S. muricatum, pepino, probably from the Andes, has leaves which are often wavy and covered with fine hair. It has purplish-blue flowers and green fruits which are later striped with purple and finally turn yellow, sweet and juicy. During the growing period water liberally and feed occasionally. Prune back in autumn and overwinter in a frost-free, cool, light place with little water and no plant food.

S. pseudocapsicum (syn. Capsicum capsicastrum), Jerusalem cherry, from Madeira, is an old-fashioned house plant. It is usually 40 cm tall and broad, with striking, orange fruits. Purchase at the end of September, beginning of October when the fruits are ripe. Place in a cool spot until Christmas at 16-18° C, and after the holiday, put back in a cool, light place. Prune back and repot in April. Sow seeds in December/January.

S. pseudocapsicum "Variegatum" has white, variegated leaves and bicoloured fruits. This plant is suitable for a sheltered, sunny or semi-shady spot. During the growing period apply liquid food once a fortnight. Prune back in spring, pruning back to one-third of the length of the stems. Repot every year at first, and every other year later on, in potting compost with clay and old cow manure.

Propagate from cuttings in summer, which take root at 20-25° C. It can also be propagated from seed.

top: Solanum rantonnetii, Nightschade

right:
Solanum pseudocapsicum, Jerusalem cherry

*Teucrium fruticans*
*Germander*

# Teucrium

*Germander*

🌱 ↕ 60-90 ◯ ✿ 7-9

*Teucrium* is widespread in temperate and moderately warm areas throughout the world, and comprises about 300 species, some of which are also indigenous in this part of the world.
These are annual, biennial or perennial herbaceous or woody-stemmed, aromatic plants with whorls of lobed, serrated, or smooth-edged leaves and whorls of flowers in the leaf axilla. They consist of a five-toothed calyx and an asymmetrical corolla with a small upper lip and much larger lower lip.
*T. fruticans* (syn. *T. latifolium*) is an erect, evergreen shrub with virtually straight stems. The young shoots and undersides of the leaves are covered with soft hair. The lanceolate leaves are 2-4 cm long, and the clusters of flowers are blue or lilac.
*T. fruticans* "Azureum" has deeper blue flowers.
This plant is suitable for a sunny spot and tolerates drought fairly well. It requires lime-rich, well-drained, sandy soil. Prune back in spring. Overwinter frost-free at 5-8° C. Propagate from seed and cuttings (September).

66

*Tibouchina urvilleana*

# Tibouchina

⚘ ↕ -2 m ⊘ ✿ 9-10(-3)

The name *Tibouchina* is derived from its popular name in Surinam. It is indigenous in tropical America and comprises 200 species. This is a woody-stemmed shrub with simple, prominently veined leaves. It has large flowers which grow singly or in groups on the young shoots.
*T. urvilleana* (syn. *T. grandiflora*, *T. semidecandra*), Glory bush, from eastern Brazil, flowers profusely. It has squarish, winged, very hairy, fragile stems, oblong, oval, 5-veined leaves, 5-10 cm long, dark green and hairy on the upper side, light green and hairy on the underside, and violet-blue flowers up to 10 cm across. It flowers from late summer, and if overwintered in a light, cool place (6-10° C), will flower until early spring.
These plants are very suitable for growing in tubs in a sunny, sheltered spot out of the wind. They need a lot of water and liquid food once a fortnight. Prune back hard in spring and repot in a nutritious mixture of leaf-mould, clay and old cow manure in well-drained pots. Propagate from stems which are not yet woody, using a growth medium.

*top: Viola's "Aalsmeerse Reuzen", Violet*

# Viola
*Violet*

• •• ○ ↕ 10-40 ◑ ◉ ❁

almost all year round

*Viola* is indigenous in temperate and mountainous regions in the tropics and subtropics, and comprises more than 500 species, mostly perennial, herbaceous plants. *V. hederacea*, ivy-leafed violet, from Australia, is not entirely winter-hardy, with runners and violet flowers, 1-1.5 cm across. It is best as a hanging plant outside in summer; overwinter in a cool, light, frost-free place.

Other species are not really suitable for growing in tubs, though they can be cultivated on a verandah or as groundcover in larger tubs, to flower early, particularly large-flowered varieties which are often cultivated to flower once. Many hybrids are derived from *V. tricolor*, e.g., "Hollandse Reuzen", which has large, single-coloured flowers, or a mixture, in spring. Propagate from seed, can be kept in a cold frame through the winter.

*V. cornuta* hybrids; different parent plants, perennial, clump-forming plants, 15-20 cm tall, suitable for a cooler, semi-shady spot. Overwinter in a fairly cool, frost-free place. If possible, propagate from cuttings.

*V. x. wittrockiana*, pansy, is usually cultivated as a biennial. It has one or several colours, often with a dark area in the middle. Suitable for a cool spot. Water liberally. Sow in early August for so-called winter violets; they flower early in spring and combine well with spring bulbs. Violets are suitable for many places with not too much bright sunlight. They require nutritious soil. Deadhead to prolong flowering period.

*left:*
*Viola x wittrockiana "Jeaunelle", Violet*

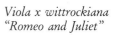

*Viola x wittrockiana*
*"Romeo and Juliet"*

*Viola x wittrockiana*
*"Aquarelle"*

*top: Yucca aloifolia "Variegata"*

# Yucca

○ ⚘ ↕ 1-3 m ↔ 1-1.5 m ○ ✳ 8-9

*Yucca* is indigenous in the southern United States and Central America. It comprises about 40 species, a number of which are cultivated in tubs. It is an evergreen, basal rosette, shrub or tree, with tough, often fibrous, sword-shaped leaves, usually serrated, and dish-shaped, white flowers in a terminal panicle, which are fragrant, especially at night.

*Y. aloifolia*, Spanish bayonet, is an upright shrub or small tree, usually with a slender trunk and compact rosettes of matt green, sharp, pointed leaves, 30-70 cm long, and panicles of flowers, 60 cm long, in late summer; *Y. aloifolia* "Variegata" has white, stripy leaves; "Marginata" has white leaf margins.

*Y. gloriosa*, Spanish dagger, is a slow-growing plant with a short, stout stem, hanging, greyish-green leaves, 60 cm long, and fragrant, creamy-white flowers with red stripes in a long panicle (up to 2.5 m long); there are various cultivars with coloured leaves.

This plant is suitable for a spot in full sunlight. Place in pots in well-drained, loamy soil, rich in humus. Water liberally in summer, and overwinter in a light, frost-free place, minimum 5° C. Propagate by removing side shoots. When the cut edge is dry, place in a pot in a mixture of sand, crumbly peat and ground-up bark.

*Yucca baccata*

*Yucca gloriosa*

A list of container plants arranged by their flowering period: see the descriptions for specific plants and information.

| Full sun: | Height (cm) | Flowering period |
|---|---|---|
| Agave | -175 | Grown for leaves |
| Isomeris | -100 | Feb-May |
| Acacia | 120-300 | Apr-May |
| Fortunella | 100-400 | Apr-Jun |
| Leptospermum | 100-300 | Apr-Jul |
| Euryops | 50-70 | May |
| Ficus | 150-450 | May |
| Citrus | 120-600 | May-Jun |
| Halimium | 50-100 | May-Jun |
| Rosmarinum | 90-150 | May-Jun |
| Cistus | -180 | May-Aug |
| Eucalyptus | -800 | May-Aug |
| Cassia | 100-200 | May-Sep |
| Fremontodendron | 300-450 | May-Sep |
| x Halimiocystus | 30-60 | May-Sep |
| Heliotropium | 30-160 | May-Sep |
| Nerium | 100-600 | May-Sep |
| Gerbera | -45 | Jun |
| Oxypetalum | -100 | Jun-Jul |
| Agapanthus | 50-150 | Jun-Aug |
| Felicia | 10-45 | Jun-Aug |
| Kunzea | 100-250 | Jun-Aug |
| Iochroma | 150-200 | Jun-Aug |
| Lupinus | 100-200 | Jun-Aug |
| Olearia | 200-450 | Jun-Aug |
| Callistemon | 100-150 | Jun-Sep |
| Clerodendrum | 200-300 | Jun-Sep |
| Echium | 40-200 | Jun-Sep |
| Erythrina | 100-200 | Jun-Sep |
| Petunia | 20-30 | Jun-Sep |
| Punica | 100-300 | Jun-Sep |
| Canna | 45-180 | Jun-Oct |
| Chrysanthemum | 30-100 | Jun-Oct |
| Mirabilis | 30-130 | Jun-Oct |
| Crinum | 30-120 | Jul-Aug |
| Teucrium | 60-90 | Jul-Sep |
| Lagerstroemia | 100-600 | Jul-Oct |
| Phygelius | 90-150 | Jul-Oct |
| Yucca | 100-300 | Aug-Sep |
| Citrus | 120-600 | Aug-Sep |
| Kochia | 60-150 | Aug-Sep |
| Leonotis | 50-180 | Aug-Sep |
| Limonium | 80-125 | Aug-Sep |
| Brugmansia | 100-500 | Aug-Oct |
| Hibiscus | 100-200 | Aug-Oct |
| Arbutus | 100-500 | Sep-Nov |
| Malvaviscus | 150-300 | Winter |

| Full sun or semi-shade: | Height (cm) | Flowering period |
|---|---|---|
| Jasminum | -200 | Mar-Jun |
| Matthiola | 30-75 | Mar-Jun |
| Buxus | 60-100 | Apr-May |
| Pelargonium | 15-200 | Apr-Oct |
| Laurus | 100-600 | May |
| Chamaerops | -100 | May-Jun |
| Rosa | 75-240 | May-Aug |
| Fuchsia | 50-150 | May-Oct |
| Cordyline | 100-200 | Jun |
| Solanum | 40-90 | Jun-Aug |
| Brassica | 20-40 | Jun-Sep |
| Lavatera | 60-150 | Jun-Sep |
| Lobelia | 10-25 | Jun-Sep |
| Phormium | 30-200 | Jul-Aug |
| Myrtus | 120-300 | Jul-Sep |
| Cestrum | 100-200 | Jul-Oct |

| Semi-shade: | Height (cm) | Flowering period |
|---|---|---|
| Eriobotrya | -250 | Grown for foliage |
| x Citrofortunella | -300 | Year-round |
| Viola | 10-40 | Year-round |
| Laurus | 100-600 | May |
| Crinodendron | 300-400 | May-Aug |
| Lantana | 30-150 | May-Sep |
| Abutilon | 60-250 | May-Oct |
| Plumbago | 100-250 | May-Oct |
| Hosta | 40-100 | Jun-Sep |
| Nandina | 100-250 | Jul |
| Fatsia | -180 | Sep-Oct |
| Tibouchina | -200 | Sep-Oct |

| Shade: | Height (cm) | Flowering period |
|---|---|---|
| Viola | 10-40 | Year-round |
| Laurus | 100-600 | May |
| Hosta | 40-100 | Jun-Sep |

*Always overwinter in a well-lit place, with little or no water.*

| Approx 5°C | | | | | Over 10°C, some water |
|---|---|---|---|---|---|
| Acacia | Fatsia | Lantana | Solanum | Felicia | Abutilon |
| Agave | Ficus | Laurus | Viola | Jasminum | Brugmansia |
| Chamaerops | Fortunella | Leonotis | Yucca | Leptospermum | Canna |
| Chrysanthemum | Fremontodendron | Limonium | | Myrtus | Cestrum |
| Cistus | Fuchsia | Lobelia | 5-10°C | Nandina | Cordyline |
| Citrus | Gerbera | Lupinus | Arbutus | Nerium | Heliotropium |
| Crinum | x Halimiocystus | Mirabilis | Brugmansia | Pelargonium | Hibiscus |
| Echium | Halimium | Olearia | Callistemon | Phormium | Malvaviscus |
| Erythrina | Iochroma | Phygelius | Cassia | Plumbago | Nerium |
| Eucalyptus | Isomeris | Punica | x Citrofortunella | Teucrium | Oxypetalum |
| Euryops | Lagerstroemia | Rosmarinum | Eriobotrya | Tibouchina | |

72

# Buying hints

The best time to buy container plants is normally from mid-March to the end of August, which is when the biggest variety are available. Prices are often at their lowest in late summer and early autumn, when garden centres need to sell off as much of their stock as possible to avoid the costs of overwintering it. Do not repot these plants until the following spring. There are also an increasing number of autumn- and winter-flowering plants available which can be used as fillers for spaces where summer-flowering plants have died back.

A good nursery or garden centre should be able to give you all the information you need about a plant's age, growth habit and cultivation requirements.

Healthy, mature plants have good leaves and bushy growth. Leafless branches or shoots will probably not grow any further.

Spots on the leaves mean something is wrong with the plant; withered leaves and a wet root ball are a sign of root damage.

### Designing a patio

When a large part of the surface of a garden is paved, this is known as a patio garden. A paved surface is normally durable and will last longer than planting. Over the years, a wide choice of hard surfacing materials has become available.

There are two types of stone: natural and artificial. Both types have their advantages and disadvantages.

Natural stones such as slate, sandstone, granite, marble and old brick have one thing in common: no two stones or tiles are identical in terms of structure, texture, colour and size. This means that the paving looks very natural, but both old and new natural stone are very expensive.

Artificial stone all looks the same as far as its size, composition and appearance are concerned. It is more affordable, and available in many different colours and sizes. It is also possible to obtain artificial but natural-looking tiles.

Square or rectangular tiles are easy to lay in straight lines and corners, but you can also use stones with seams which can be broken in half along their length or width.

Whichever material you use, it will need a hard, stable surface of well-firmed hardcore or chippings 6 to 8 cm thick, covered with a 5-cm layer of sharp sand. This needs to be bedded down well, either mechanically, or by treading down or generous watering. A fixed edge will stop the surface from spreading.

If you place a layer of mortar over this hard surface, and lay the tiles with or without joins, the patio will be watertight. The surface will need to slope slightly away from the centre so that the water runs off it.

# Planting

*Tubs, pots and troughs*
*Containers can be bought in a huge variety of sizes, shapes and materials. The two main guiding principles are that the pot should match the plant, and both should fit into the design as a whole.*
*Size How big the pot is will depend on the size and age of the plant. The plant will sometimes have to grow for years in the same container, so growing plants will regularly need to be transferred into a larger pot.*
*Shape The container needs to be both stable and attractive; a large opening at the top makes it easier to repot plants. Unattractive pots can be covered in natural material or placed in a larger pot holder.*
*Material Terracotta is available in all shapes and sizes, and has a natural appearance, but is heavy, breakable and relatively expensive. Wooden containers have a neutral, smart appearance, but are expensive and prone to decay. Plastic will not weather like other materials, and is lightweight and affordable, but in most cases it is less easy on the eye.*

Using plants in tubs and pots has one big advantage: it gives you a choice of varieties which are not normally hardy enough to go in the garden. But they will flourish in summer on a patio or in a sheltered place: these are the true container or orangery plants. Of course countless plants are grown in containers, but bear in mind that because they have limited space they are usually less vigorous than in the open soil. In fact all plants which can be left outside in summer and kept in a frost-free place in winter are known as container plants.

The choice of plants will depend on the position of the garden (whether or not it is sunny) and the amount of care they need. It is vital that you feed and water them regularly.

A well-grown container plant will not get enough water even in a summer downpour, and has limited access to nutrients.

Match the containers to the plants, perhaps using brightly-coloured pot to enliven a plant with grey foliage, or using pots or flowers which echo the background colours. The shape and size of the pot will partly determine the shape and size of the plant.

If you have limited space available, hanging pots may be the answer. Also, standard-grown plants take up less space than bushy ones. If the garden has any steps, use these for containers, provided they are wide enough. If you place a group of pots against a wall or fence, put the tallest plants at the back and the lower and trailing varieties more to the front so that they form a harmonious whole.

In some cases, a raised bed may give a closer view of combinations of ground-cover plants such as ivy *(Hedera)*, periwinkle *(Vinca)* and forget-me-nots *(Myosotis)*.

If you place tubs on a balcony or roof garden, you will need to take account of the total weight of the container, soil and plants, which may be considerable.

Herbs are particularly suited to ceramic containers, and aquatic and bog plants can be grown in an ordinary pot standing in a shallow dish of water.

Most true aquatic plants need a depth of at least 30 cm, and will grow best in pond compost. They should not be placed in full sun, because too much heat will cause algae to grow. Many annuals, such as *Lobelia, Nemophila* and *Viola*, small succulents such as *Sedum* and *Sempervivum*, and small bulbous plants such as *Muscari* and tulips look good in containers, particularly in combination with small standard-grown shrubs.

It is often easier to put the empty tub or pot in place first and then add the soil and plant it. You will need a trolley on wheels or something similar to move containers once they have been filled.

## Maintenance
### Autumn and winter
Most plants should be given brought indoors in mid-October, before the first frost, though depending on the weather, some can be left outside for a few more weeks. Clean the pots well, removing any slugs or snails, and do not put them indoors when they are wet, as they

will dry slowly because of the low temperature. If you regularly air them on fine days, this will help to prevent fungal diseases. Keep the plants fairly dry over winter, and do not feed them. A number of plants can be overwintered outdoors if the pot or tub is protected from frost. Evergreen shrubs such as *Buxus*, some ornamental grasses, evergreen ferns and ornamental cabbages, most conifers and early spring bulbs can be left outdoors.

### Spring
As the temperature rises, so the plants will need to be regularly aired to prevent temperature differences. Remove dead leaves and early runners. In April, repot and if necessary prune or trim the smaller plants, beginning with those that can go outside first.

In mid-May, when frost is no longer likely, the more tender plants can also be taken outside; do this on a cloudy, if possible somewhat rainy day. Do not immediately place the plants in full sun, as there is a risk of leaf scorch. Evergreen plants will then often lose their older leaves; this is normal.

Summer
The microclimate in a patio garden may be much warmer than in an ordinary garden. Plants on paving or beside a wall will benefit from the reflected heat, as will those grown on a trellis against a wall. In this situation, their water consumption will be much higher, so you may have to water them twice a day, once in the early morning and once at dusk. Use an adjustable hose nozzle to make sure they receive the proper amount of water. Where small plants have dried out, plunge their root balls in water to revive them.
Feed plants regularly until the end of August. Keep them neat with occasional extra trimming, and dead-head flowering plants unless you want them to fruit or set seed, bearing in mind that plants from warmer climes rarely do so in a temperate climate like ours.
In urban areas, acid rain may acidify the soil in containers; bear this in mind when feeding the plants, except for acid-loving plants such as *Rhododendron*.

## Repotting and pruning
Plants should ideally be repotted at the end of their dormant period. Unless otherwise stated, use potting compost with a little dried cow manure in smaller tubs and pots.
Use garden soil for larger containers: three parts of soil with one part of potting compost on top. Potting compost contains the nutrients the plants need and is worth the extra expense. Mixing with peat improves the soil structure and its water and air retention, but does not add any nutrients.
In most cases, plants can be pruned at the same time as they are repotted. Always use sharp, clean equipment. Early-flowering plants should be pruned immediately after they have flowered; later-flowering ones just before the end of the dormant period. Plants should normally be pruned so that they taper towards the top: this maximises the amount of light that falls on the leaves and prevents the plant from becoming top-heavy.
To encourage bushy growth, pinch out the growing tips regularly. In the case of plants such as *Fuchsia*, remove every third pair of leaves a number of times during the growing season; this only takes a few minutes per plant.

## Propagation
*Layering:* Choose a fairly young branch near the base of the shrub. Bend it down to the ground and peg it to the soil 15 cm from the tip using a loop of wire. After a few months, the branch will have rooted and can be separated from the parent plant.
*Cuttings:* Root non-flowering shoot tips about 10 cm long in a mixture of peat dust, sharp sand and a little potting compost (a heel cutting is a section of the stem with a piece of bark from the parent plant). Use hormone powder to encourage rooting.
*Division:* Prise the root ball apart so that each section has some roots and one or more healthy shoots.
*From seed:* Follow the instructions in the descriptions of individual plants.

## Pests and diseases
Moving container plants indoors and outdoors can increase the chance of pests and diseases, but many of these problems can be prevented by proper winter care. Use biodegradable chemical sprays, or one of the many home-made remedies. Spider mite and aphids can be washed off using a jet of water from a hose, though make sure the plant can take this battering, and ensure that you also spray the undersides of the leaves. Aphids can also be killed using a mixture of 20 grammes of washing-up liquid and 10 millilitres of methylated spirits to a litre of water. Woolly aphids can be prevented by carefully but thoroughly washing the roots when you repot the plant.
*Citrus* and *Fortunella* may suffer from iron deficiency. The best remedy is to allow some nails to rust in water for a few weeks, or water with a few grammes of iron chelates to a litre of water.

Most European countries have associations specialising in growing one particular kind of plant, and these can be a useful source of specialist knowledge. There is also a wide-ranging literature on container plants.

# Small workers in the garden

### Life around plants in tubs and on patios
*On balconies, patios and roof gardens, plants in tubs provide greenery close at hand: a touch of nature in the middle of the concrete urban jungle. Insects are attracted by all the elements of this exotic beauty - oleander, yucca or laurel: bees and bumblebees. The drinks we have to refresh ourselves on hot summer days also bring out the wasps. Most people are none too keen on wasps. Fortunately, the wasp season does not last long; it takes place in late summer.*

Wasp, *Vespula vulgaris*

## Wasps

In broad terms, the life cycle of the wasp is the same as that of the bee. The females who were fertilized in the previous season and have survived the winter, awake from their hibernation in spring. One female becomes the mother and queen of an entire wasp colony; she immediately starts to look for a suitable nesting place. A sheltered corner in a shed or under the roof will do very well. The queen builds the nest with wood fibres which she chews with her powerful jaws to produce a sort of papier-maché. Straw mats form perfect raw material. The wasp colony is hatched from the eggs which are deposited in the cells of the strong, light nest. In summer, the wasps buzz around the patio or balcony, searching for their favourite food: sweet things and meat - just like flies. Finally the autumn rains and first night frost put an end to virtually all the wasps' lives. The wasp does not have many enemies other than the inclemency of the weather, apart from one small bird which is seen increasingly often, even in small gardens, the flycatcher.

Flycatcher,
Ficedula hypoleuca

## Flycatchers

These birds are steadily increasing their territory. They are taking advantage of the many nesting boxes which have been put out in recent years, where they like to breed. The best way to identify a flycatcher is to see how these quick little birds catch insects. Looking dapper, they sit on a branch or a fence, and then suddenly shoot off to catch the passing prey from the air. They rarely miss, although they sometimes have to perform the most capricious tricks. Their diet also includes wasps. They are immune to the odd sting, but to prevent being stung, the wasp's sting is wiped on a branch with lightning speed. This is necessary, because unlike the sting of a bee or bumble bee, the wasp's sting does not have a barb and does not stay in the victim's body. The wasp can continue to use it all its life, as often as it likes. Flycatchers know what to do with wasps, but they have their own enemies. Obviously this includes the neighbour's cat, but there is also a fast and dangerous bird of prey: the sparrowhawk.

Sparrowhawk,
Accipiter nisus

## Sparrowhawk

The sparrowhawk is the only bird of prey found in smaller gardens. This predator likes gardens, and specialises in catching small birds. It surprises them by suddenly making a low dive and swooping quickly over hedges and shrubs. It obstinately pursues its prey, often between the branches of a tree and buildings. Eventually the sparrowhawk usually succeeds in making the kill. In this way the food chain passes from the fly eaten by the wasp to the bird of prey which has consumed the flycatcher.

## List of symbols

|  |  |
|--------|-------------|
| ▪ (single dot in box) | annual |
| ▪▪ (two dots in box) | biennial |
| ○ (circle in box) | perennial |
| (bulb symbol) | bulbous plant |
| (tuber symbol) | tuberous plant |
| (tree symbol) | tree |
| (shrub symbol) | shrub |
| ↕ (vertical arrow) | height in cm |
| ↔ (horizontal arrow) | breadth in cm |
| ○ (open circle) | full sunlight |
| (half-shaded circle) | semi-shade |
| (shaded circle) | shade |
| (flower symbol) | flowering months |
| ❋ (snowflake) | winter-hardy |
| ! | poisonous |
| ✂ (scissors) | suitable for cut flowers |
| (berry symbol) | berry |
| (watering can, full) | keep moist at all times, compost should not dry out |
| (watering can, half) | keep moderately moist, compost may dry out slightly |
| (watering can, empty) | keep fairly dry, only water during growing period |
| (spray symbol) | spray, avoid spraying when plant is flowering |